TESLA:
THE FORGOTTEN GENIUS
OF ELECTRICITY

⚡

James Samuels

NMD Books
Simi Valley, CA

Copyright 2016 – James Samuels

All rights reserved. No part of this book may be reproduced in any format or by any means without written permission from the publisher.

Library of Congress Cataloging-in-Publication
Tesla the Forgotten Genius of Electricity by James Samuels
ISBN: 978-1-936828-45-6(Softcover)

First Edition March 2016

CHAPTER 1

ON JANUARY 9, 1861, many events occurred which were to reshape the history of the world. In America, the opening gun of the Civil War sounded the warning of the bloody years to follow. In Germany, young Bismarck, who was to be Germany's first Chancellor, and responsible for the militarization of the Fatherland, received his first decoration. In England, Queen Victoria was forging into a unified whole the far flung British Empire and casting knowing eyes upon the Suez Canal, which had been started the previous year.

In the little town of Smiljan in the Serbian province of Lika, then known as Croatia, a seemingly unimportant event took place which, too, was destined to shape the future. Nikola Tesla, scarcely five years old, found the family's pet poodle Trixie dying. The little black poodle was lying under a bush at the side of the road, whimpering, and the small boy picked her up and carried her home to his twelve-year-old brother Dane. Strangely, the death of that pet dog was to be the first of several events that would determine the course of Nikki Tesla's life.

Trixie had been given to Dane by one of their father's congregation. Everyone in Smiljan liked the Tesla family. The Reverend Milutin Tesla was a tall, handsome man with a fine speaking voice and a prodigious memory. He knew the Bible by heart and could quote it word for word in proof of a point he might be trying to make. Djouka, his wife, a charming, attractive woman, also had an amazing memory. She had learned to speak German, French, and Italian, as well as her native Serbian, even though she never learned to read or write.

Milka, Angelina, and Dane were the three oldest children; Nikola and little Marica were the youngest; and all pleasant, well mannered, and charming to be with. Neighbors often visited the Tesla home for an evening of music or conversation, but it was Dane they talked about at their dinner tables or in their living rooms. Some said he was a genius; others were sure that he was not long for this world. Everyone agreed that, at twelve, Dane knew more than most of the grownups in Smiljan.

No one was surprised when he was given a present of a thoroughbred French poodle, even though he already owned a big white and tan dog, part Spitz and part Collie, which he had found in the woods behind the rectory. The family had accepted Keno, but no one thought him very smart. Certainly he was not beautiful.

Trixie was both and Dane spent every minute of his spare time teaching her tricks. She learned quickly and soon the evening visits to the Tesla home were even more enlivened by a "show" that Dane often put on. Trixie would walk on her hind legs, sit up and beg, fetch, and "speak," performing all her tricks with such relish and obvious enjoyment that the guests could not fail to praise the young boy for his kindness and patience as a trainer.

When Nikki brought the dying Trixie home, the whole family gathered around anxiously. Dane turned angrily on his little brother. "What did you do to her?" he cried.

"Dane!" The Reverend Tesla spoke sharply. "Nikki didn't do anything. Why should he?"

"Because he hates her," Dane answered. "He's angry because no one pays any attention to him since we got Trixie."

"Stop such talk at once, Dane!" Mrs. Tesla ordered, putting her arm around the bewildered little boy. "Nikki loves the dog as much as you do." She knelt beside the little dog. "Get me the white of an egg, Angelina. Quickly!"

They did everything that could be done, but it was no use. Nikki, seeing the little dog's eyes glaze over and close, felt very sorry for her, but even sorrier for his older brother. As he reached out to take Dane's hand, Keno arrived, late as usual, and pushed his big, bumbling way between them. He walked over to where the little black dog lay, nuzzled her, and licked her nose. Getting no response, he raised troubled eyes to his master's face. Dane looked down at him and cried out more in grief than in anger:

"Why did it have to happen to Trixie? Why did Trixie have to die?"

Keno's long, plumed tail drooped and he slunk away.

"You shouldn't have said that," Nikki protested. "He thinks you're angry at him."

Dane stared at his brother a few moments before answering, then said, "I didn't mean it the way you think. I only meant that, when there are so many dogs in the village, why did it have to be Trixie?"

Nikki silently accepted this explanation, but he knew that, for a moment, his brother had wished that Keno had died instead of Trixie.

After that, Nikki seemed to change. He became shy and withdrawn, as if afraid to call attention to himself, and this was especially noticeable whenever Dane was present. Perhaps, in time, he would have forgotten the unhappy episode of the dog and his brother's harsh accusations had not unexpected tragedy stricken the Tesla household.

No one knew exactly how it happened. All five of the children were playing in the back yard when suddenly there was a loud scream. Mrs. Tesla found Dane, writhing in pain, at the foot of the stone cellar steps. He lost consciousness when they carried him to the upstairs room he shared with Nikki, but he soon came to and began to talk excitedly, saying that Nikki had pushed him. The Reverend and Mrs. Tesla did not for one moment believe that their youngest had deliberately set out to hurt his older brother, but they didn't want him to hear Dane's delirious accusations and become upset, so it was decided that Nikola should spend a week or two with some friends who lived nearby, and little Marica went with him to Mr. and Mrs. Mark Wentzlas' to keep him company.

Every morning Mrs. Wentzlas got Nikki his breakfast and hustled him off to school. And every day, when he returned at noontime, she was watching for him from the great bay window at the front of the little farmhouse. She would wave at him and little Marica would come bouncing out the front door, while Keno galumphed from somewhere at the back of the house to stand with his forepaws on the white gate waiting for Nikki to pat him.

But one day Nikki came home to find only Mrs. Wentzlas waiting at the gate, with Keno standing quietly at her side.

"I have sad news for you, Nikki," she said. "You must be a big, brave boy."

He looked up at her worn, kind face and saw that her eyes were red, as if she had been crying. Even before she spoke he guessed what she was going to say.

"Dane has gone away," she said solemnly and Nikki nodded. He had known she was going to say that. Why was it, he wondered, that grownups so often said someone had "gone away" or "passed on" when they meant "died"? When an animal died, they said so, but it seemed as if people didn't ever die— they just "went away."

"I knew you wouldn't cry." Mrs. Wentzlas went on. "I knew you'd be a fine, brave boy. And now you just go into the kitchen and wash and then go upstairs. You'll find your Sunday suit laid out on your bed."

"Do I have to wear stockings?" Nikki asked.

"Of course. All your parents' friends and neighbors—everybody who loved Dane—will be there to say 'goodbye' to him. Now hurry along. Marica is already dressed. We'll go over to your house as soon as you're ready."

Obediently Nikki washed at the pump in the kitchen, then went up the back stairs to his room and dressed quickly. As he was coming down the front stairs he suddenly heard Mrs. Wentzlas speaking:

"—didn't cry or seem to feel anything at all. Seemed almost stupid."

Then a rumble. That was Mr. Wentzlas talking.

"Oh, I know he's only five years old," Mrs. Wentzlas answered impatiently, "but he's no genius. Oh Mark, why did it have to be Dane?"

Nikki stood frozen on the dark stairway. Suddenly he wanted his mother. He wanted her arms around him. He wanted to hear her say that she didn't feel that way too. But what if she did? Almost as if in answer to his thoughts, Mrs. Wentzlas continued: "Oh, I know I shouldn't have said that, or even thought it, but I can't help it. Dane would have grown up to be a great man. He would have brought honor to his parents and to Smiljan . . ."

Nikki forgot his own hurt and felt suddenly very sorry for his mother and father. And then, right there on the dark stair way, he made his decision. He would be a greater, more important man than Dane would have been! He would bring more fame and greater honor to his parents than his brother would ever have brought!

Mrs. Wentzlas' voice grew louder. "Whatever can be keeping that boy? We'll be late unless . . . Oh, there you are!"

She had come out into the hall and now she held out her hand to him. "Come, Nikki. We must hurry."

As they went down the walk toward the gate, Keno appeared from behind the house, walking slowly as if he knew that it would not be appropriate to jump and frisk about. Nikki wondered if he knew about Dane.

"You be a good dog, Keno," Mrs. Wentzlas said. "You stay and guard the house. We won't be gone long."

"Can't Keno come?" Nikki asked in surprise.

"Certainly not," Mrs. Wentzlas answered firmly.

"But why not? You said that people who loved Dane were coming to say goodbye to him. Keno loved him. Can't he say goodbye to him too?"

Mr. and Mrs. Wentzlas looked at each other.

"The boy's right," Mr. Wentzlas rumbled.

Mrs. Wentzlas stooped down and gave Nikki a quick little hug.

"Of course, you're right," she said. "Keno can come along."

Keno took his place beside Nikki and they went through the gate and on down the street side by side, the dog ignoring the taunting chatter of the chipmunks in the low branches of the elms that lined the sidewalk—resisting a temptation to reply to the challenge that at any other time would have been irresistible. After they had gone a short distance and were out of earshot of the others, Nikki addressed the dog seriously:

"Keno, I am going to train you. I'm going to be a better dog trainer than Dane was, and you're going to be the smartest, best trained dog in the whole world."

Keno waved his plume slowly back and forth without much enthusiasm.

"You don't believe it, do you?" Nikki went on. "Well, you'll see. Everybody will come to our house to watch us do tricks. Everybody will talk about you. You'll be famous! Just wait and see"

Secretly and with intense concentration and singleness of purpose that would have been startling—almost frightening— to anyone who might have seen them, Nikki spent every free moment training the big dog. Responding to this unexpected windfall of patient and affectionate attention, the friendly animal was transformed from a clumsy, lumbering clown into a skilled performer. And, as Nikki had prophesied, the night finally did arrive when neighbors and friends, who had dropped in to enjoy an evening of music and conversation with the Teslas in an effort to help them forget their loss, found themselves unexpected witnesses to a performance they had never dreamed of. Keno walked on his forelegs, balanced a piece of sugar on his nose and then tossed it in the air on the command of his new young master. Keno fetched and "spoke" and played hide and seek and did many tricks that they had never seen a dog do before.

But being a better dog trainer than Dane was not enough. Nikki felt impelled to do something startling, something unusual, but he had no idea what it would be. It was his mother's ingenuity and handiness with tools that finally gave him the idea of becoming an inventor. Mrs. Tesla had created several convenient or laborsaving devices for home use: the fourfold screen that served as a partition between the children's beds and provided a modicum of privacy, and her "eggbeater."

She had tied two wooden forks together, facing each other, finding it much easier to beat eggs thoroughly with this device than with a single fork. One day Mrs. Tesla complained that her wrists ached, and said she wished she could think of something that would turn her eggbeater.

"The amount of energy I waste beating eggs for this family could probably pull a cart from here to Prague!" she said laughingly.

Nikki pricked up his ears. If he could think of something that would turn the forks, he would be doing something that Dane had never thought of. If only he could think of something! He thought about it a great deal, but when the idea finally came to him, it was while he was teaching Keno a new trick and not thinking about the eggbeater at all.

Not far from the Tesla home a mountain stream rushed through the woods, tumbling over itself as it raced downhill over small rocks and tree roots. Nikki decided that the power of the water should be used to turn something that would in turn cause a gear to revolve. The gear could be connected to a small upright post that would be turned by pulleys. In his mind the upright post represented his mother's eggbeater. He remembered that when the woodcutters chopped down some of the huge trees on the mountainside, they often sawed the trunks into round segments that could be used as small cartwheels. He went in search of a discarded or broken one and succeeded in finding a round one that had obviously been sawed too thin to serve any practical purpose, for it was only about an inch thick.

Happily, Nikki bored a hole in the center of it, pushed a long green stick through the hole, and rested its two ends in crotched sticks he drove into the soft ground on either bank of the stream. As soon as the water struck the rough perimeter of the circular wooden segment, it began to revolve very slowly around the stick. Nikki saw at once that the water power was not great enough to turn the stick as well as the wheel. He would have to find a place where the waters rushed with greater force—perhaps he could find a waterfall nearby, then he could run pulleys down the hill right into the Tesla kitchen. By connecting them with the eggbeater, the water power would turn it without any help from his mother.

Accompanied by the seemingly tireless Keno, Nikki fell into the habit of taking long hikes into the nearby hills in search of a waterfall.

The Reverend Tesla was pleased that his son should find so much of interest in nature, and Mrs. Tesla often made up picnic lunches for him to take on his trips.

It was on one of these hikes into the mountains that Nikki came upon a very old and long forgotten chapel formed by a great bronze door that had been hinged with iron spikes into a boulder that had fallen in front of the opening of a cave. Beyond the partly open door he could see the cavern, which was dark and evil smelling, but his curiosity and his adventurous spirit overcame his fear. Calling to Keno to precede him, he started toward the cave entrance. Something, however, seemed to frighten the dog, and for the first time since Dane's death he refused to obey Nikki's command.

"Keno!" Nikki shouted. "Go in!"

But the dog backed away, the hair bristling along the length of his spine, his lips curled back from his teeth in a soundless snarl.

"Sissy! Fraidycat!" Nikki jeered, but Keno would not approach the cave.

"All right then, I'll go in alone," the boy said and crawled around the heavy door and entered the cavern. The contact of his shoulder as he brushed by the door was just enough to dislodge the rust encrusted hinge. The door sagged and the top swung across the opening, completely blocking it. Nikki was sealed in the total darkness of the damp smelling stone chapel. He threw his weight against the door in sudden panic, but his efforts did not even make it budge. From the other side the frightened boy could hear the faint sound of the dog's barking.

"Go home, Keno!" Nikki shouted. "Go home and get help." Keno did just that. Hours later, panting and bedraggled, he galloped into the Tesla yard.

"What's the matter, Keno? What's all the fuss about?" Mrs. Tesla asked. He paid no attention to her but ran through the house, quite obviously searching for something or someone. He almost hurtled out of the front door and raced along the wooden sidewalk to the church. As he reached it, the Reverend Tesla emerged from a small side door and the frenzied dog flung himself upon the minister, barking and whimpering, running away for a short distance and then returning to the man.

After watching for a moment the Reverend Tesla asked, "You want me to go with you? Is that it, boy?" and Keno barked furiously. Mr.

Wentzlas heard the noise and came hurrying along the street. "What's the matter, Reverend?" he asked.

"I believe the dog wants to take me to Nikki," the Reverend Tesla answered slowly, and Keno bounded about, as if to show his relief at being understood.

"What are we waiting for?" Mr. Wentzlas cried, and both of them started out after the barking dog. Four other neighbors, hearing the commotion, joined the party and headed for the mountains with Keno leading the way. It took all the strength of the six men to swing the heavy bronze door away from the opening far enough to let the Reverend Tesla slip through and carry out the now unconscious Nikki. They revived him and the little procession turned homeward.

"What were you doing 'way up here on the mountainside, Nikki?" his father asked him.

"I was looking for a waterfall."

"From now on you'll have to be more careful when you going to the woods," his father said sternly, but Nikki noticed a warm smile quivering on the lips that were barely visible beneath the handlebar mustache.

"I'll try, Nikki promised.

They walked down the steep mountain path in silence for a time, Mr. Wentzlas and the other neighbors following behind the Reverend Tesla.

"Papa," Nikki said, "I don't have to stop thinking about the water, do I?"

His father stared at him, completely puzzled. "Water? What water?"

"Water all over—everywhere. The rivers and streams and brooks—all moving and none of them doing anybody any good."

"Nonsense," the Reverend Tesla replied. "Of course they do good. They supply moisture for our gardens; they provide fish and other food for people to eat."

"I didn't mean that," Nikki tried to explain. "I only meant that their force is being wasted. If somebody could capture it —the way my water wheel does—and use it to help people turn things and move things and . . ."

The Reverend Tesla laughed. "One inventor in the family is enough! Oh, I'll admit that the four way screen that your mother thought up, with the hinges on both sides, has its good points. It does keep the heat from the stove away from the kitchen table whenever we decide to eat there instead of in the dining room. And the bed without legs that your mother made is easier to get into, instead of climbing up into the big four-poster—but we're the ones who have to test all these experiments, and if you were to begin too, there's no telling what we'd find ourselves doing!"

"I'm going to capture the water's power," Nikki said stubbornly. "I'm going to harness it the way Mr. Wentzlas harnesses old Meg."

The Reverend Tesla looked down at his fivefold son's thin, earnest face and a frown of worry wrinkled his forehead. "Don't try too hard," he cautioned.

"I'm going to make you proud of me. Papa," the boy said.

"We like you the way you are."

Then Niki said something that made no sense at all to his father: "Dane liked Keno the way he was."

Had the Reverend Tesla asked Nikki what he meant, he might have understood what forces drove his son on to endless and tireless efforts to succeed, but he saw no particular meaning behind Nikki's words. He thought the boy was criticizing the son he had lost, and so he spoke impatiently and said exactly the wrong thing:

"Dane was different, he was a genius."

Nikki decided in that moment that he would invent something that would startle the world.

CHAPTER 2

NIKKI tried one thing after another with a sort of desperate compulsion that made him seem almost feverish. Both the Reverend Tesla and his wife sensed that the boy was under a strain, but neither of them guessed the cause. Meanwhile Nikki invented a blowgun and soon afterward a popgun, which he sold to his classmates in elementary school. When an epidemic of broken windows struck Smiljan, Nikki realized that this was not an invention that was likely to raise him in the esteem of their neighbors.

Just after his fifth birthday he made his first attempt to emu late the flight of a bird. The result was three broken ribs and six weeks in bed. Then followed another approach to the water wheel. This time he used parts of a toy cart and made scoops which turned the wheel much more effectively than had the water on the relatively smooth surface of his first wheel. Us continued to drive himself, and grew thinner and quieter as time passed.

"It's almost as if he blames himself for Dane's death," Mrs. Tesla said. "You don't suppose he overheard those delirious mutterings our boy . . ."

"No," her husband assured her. "I'm sure Nikola doesn't blame himself. Perhaps he's just trying to make up to us for our loss."

"Try to get him to relax, Milutin," Mrs. Tesla urged. "The boy will make himself sick."

When the Reverend Tesla's popularity and many services to both church and community were rewarded by a promotion to a much larger parish in the thriving city of Go spic, his parents thought the move would be good for Nikki. The boy, now seven, was delighted at the prospect of moving to a new home. His disappointment was great when he finally saw the redbrick rectory and the huge Gothic church adjoining it. He had spent a happy childhood close to nature, and he disliked the city with its little houses all crowded together like sheep huddled in a corral before a thunderstorm. Nor did he like the people he met. His reserve did not permit him to make friends easily and his loneliness added further to his unhappiness.

It was his job to ring the church bell before and after services. After a service one Sunday in the \ spring, Nikki came down the spiral staircase in great leaps, swinging himself past three or four steps by leverage on the handrail. At the bottom of the stairway he sprang down and landed on the train of the new gown of the Countess con Filibustering—the wife of the fat Austrian mayor of Go spic With the sound of tearing cloth, the very pompous dowager was bereft of her skirt and her dignity. Her face purple with rage, she turned to the astonished minister.

"This boy is your son, is he not, Dr. Tesla?" she asked accusingly. The Reverend Tesla nodded.

"I want him punished, and punished severely," the angry woman ordered. "He has been rude and destructive. I want—"

"He meant no harm," Nikki's father protested. "Perhaps it was wrong for him to jump in the House of the Lord, but—"

"Perhaps!!" she screamed. "Perhaps? Of course it was wrong and I want him punished. And I want the damages paid for. Do you understand?"

"Calm yourself. Madam," the Reverend Tesla replied quietly." The damages will be paid."

"Out of what? The measly salary we pay you to preach in our church? It would take a year."

"You will have to be patient then, for I have not yet received .even the first quarterly payment of the 'measly salary' the church pays me. But if you will send me a bill, it will be paid."

"Very well," the Countess sputtered, not at all mollified by the minister's quiet tone, "but you must promise to punish the boy." '

"The boy will not be punished."

"What?"

"He was guilty of nothing more serious than an excess of high spirits. It was an accident. I'm certain that Nikola is very sorry for what happened. I cannot find it in my heart to feel that he requires further punishment."

"My husband and I are not accustomed to having our requests refused. I say that the boy must be taught manners and respect—if not for persons at least for the church.

"The Bishop shall hear of this" the Countess con Furstenburg threatened. "We'll see what he thinks of your disrespect." She swept the remains of her torn gown about her and moved naughtily out onto the marble steps at the church entrance.

Dr. Tesla looked down at his small son and smiled. "Let us go home together," he said.

"Oh Papa!" Nikki cried. "Can't we go back to Smiljan, where everyone was friendly?"

"I'm afraid not." His father said and explained that a new minister had already been installed in the church there and could not very well be asked to give up his post.

"We'll just have to be brave—all of us," he said.

At that moment Nikki wished that he had the words to tell his father how sorry he was for what he had done and how much he admired him for his kindness and his loyalty.

He soon found out that being brave was not easy. The On Burgomasters had two sons and a daughter at the school that Nikki attended. The girl talked to her friends about the Teslas and made it plain that her parents would be pleased if so crude a family were ignored and socially ostracized. These were only words to Nikki and did not really hurt him. But the two boys did not confine their dislike to words. Nikki discovered that if he managed to think hard enough about something else, he didn't feel the pain so much when they pulled his hair or twisted his arm back between his shoulder blades. When the bullies finally learned that they couldn't make him knuckle under to them, they decided to leave Nikki alone; but while this afforded some physical relief, it did not help to make the boy happy. Then when the Teslas had been in Go spic little more than a year, Nikola was given an opportunity to win recognition and a sort of grudging respect.

The Town Council decided to purchase a brand new fire engine, which turned out to be a most impressive looking contraption. The Council was very proud of it and planned a parade and a public demonstration to introduce it to the enthusiastic townspeople. General Count con Furstenburg, husband of the formidable lady whose wrath Nikki had incurred, had volunteered to arrange for the purchase of the new apparatus, and on the day of the carefully planned ceremony stood in the place of honor, a hastily erected rotunda on the river bank, where the shiny new engine was to be demonstrated.

Pompously and at great length the Count told the assembled citizens how very fortunate they were to have such a splendid Town Council headed by so distinguished a leader as himself. He pointed out the vast improvement of the new apparatus over the old bucket brigade system and explained at length how it was made and operated. It seemed to Nikki, standing shyly at the outermost edge of the crowd, that the Mayor had done everything but draw a diagram of what seemed like a very simple idea. The long, flat canvas hose that led from the engine to the river was the means of drawing the water into the tank, the central supply source, from which it would be pumped, under pressure, onto the flames.

At last the pompous little man stopped lecturing and called upon sixteen members of the Volunteer Fire Department to man the pump handles. Then, to the amazed delight of the onlookers, eight men on each side grasped the two long handles and began a sort of formal minuet. The pump was operated much as a railroad handcar is operated, first one then the other handle being forced down. A silence fell upon the crowd as they stared in fascination, waiting for the shining brass nozzle to begin spouting an impressive stream of water skyward—but Nikki only had eyes for the sixteen men who seemed to be bowing to one another over the heavy pump handles.

"Nikki!" his mother said sharply. "Stop smiling. They'll think you're laughing at them. Haven't you caused us enough trouble without making them any angrier?"

Nikola obeyed instantly, and a look of hurt appeared in his eyes. Mrs. Tesla, seeing the pained look, felt sorry for her sharp words and put her around his shoulder.

"I'm sorry, Nikki," she said gently, "I know you never mean to cause trouble. It just seems to follow you around like Keno."

Then, completely forgetting her warning to her son, Mrs. Tesla laughed too. It was indeed amusing to watch the sixteen men laboring in vain—their almost mystic genuflections producing nothing.

The Count angrily ordered the men to pump harder, but their resultant perspiration was the only moisture forthcoming. Suddenly, without understanding how, Nikola knew that there was nothing wrong with the new apparatus. He realized that the men would not be pulling and pushing against so much pressure it water were entering the hose. Therefore, the trouble must be at the river end. Without a word he ducked quickly from under his mother's arm and ran toward the river bank, taking off his clothes as he went.

Stripped down to his long woolen drawers, he held his nose and leaped from the high bank. He saw immediately that the mouth of the hose had folded back upon itself and was flattened by the vacuum created by the pumping. Holding his breath and using both hands with all his strength, Nikki flipped the hose over and saw the water rush in. He immediately surfaced.

Under the continued bellowing of the purple faced Mayor, the sixteen members of the Volunteer Fire Department of the city of Go spic continued to bow to each other rhythmically as they pumped, but the men holding the hose gazed with considerable interest at Mrs. Tesla as she and some of her neighbors ran fearfully toward the spot where Nikki had jumped into the river. In their curiosity, the firemen permitted the nozzle of the hose to droop down.

At that precise moment the water released by Nikola and pumped by the conscientious volunteers belched from the nozzle in a mighty sixty foot stream, exactly as the Count con Furstenburg had said it would! But he had claimed that it would shoot sixty feet straight up in the air. Actually, with the hose aimed at the speakers' platform, the water blasted the Mayor and three members of the Council right off their chairs and onto the floor.

"Turn it up! Up in the air, you idiots!" On Furstenburg shouted as soon as he could get enough breath with which to shout. "Turn it away. I'll have you all discharged for this!"

But the firemen, watching the growing crowd at the riverbank, were paying no attention. The vice chairman of the Council helped the Count to his feet and whispered to him, "Whoever fixed the apparatus deserves to be rewarded. I'd rather be a little wet from the hose than have had to face the crowd another minute if it hadn't worked."

On Furstenburg decided that it would be wise to laugh at his own discomfort. "You're absolutely right!" he announced.

Those of the Go spic citizenry who lined the bank of the little river were impressed by the little drama they had witnessed. Eager hands were held out to the skinny, nearly naked boy who, now that his object had been achieved, was realizing the risk he had taken to achieve it. Nikola was hauled up onto dry land, embraced by his weeping mother, and hoisted onto the shoulders of the shouting, laughing firemen. They carried him to a place of honor on their recent acquisition, wrapped coats around him, and wheeled the bright new engine and pump down the main streets of Go spic in a march of triumph in Nikki's honor. The young boy was happy at last because he had helped to make his father's job secure '

CHAPTER 3

WHEN HE WAS NINE and in his last year of elementary school, called Normal School, in Serbia, Nikola temporarily abandoned the study of water power for renewed work on the development of air power. He still wanted to invent something that would impress grownups, particularly his parents. One day, although not conscious of thinking about it, he suddenly pictured a way to create a motor that would rotate his mother's eggbeater without using up her energy.

He visualized a small wheel revolving parallel to the ground and meshing with a gear that was connected to an upright pole. When the wheel turned, it turned the gears, and they in turn made the pole revolve. And the wheel, he thought, would be much easier to turn than the pole. Wind or air could be used to turn a small light wheel. He thought about ways to create air power. For two years he had held a healthy respect for the power caused by the napping wings of the great hawks that flew over the cornfields from time to time. He well remembered his broken ribs after an attempt to fly from the barn roof, with only his mother's parasol to serve as wings. He had learned then (hat the sustaining power of a bird's wing was far greater than he had thought!

He had a sudden flash of inspiration: he would use bugs as a source of power! After capturing a jarful of June bugs, Nikki retired to the privacy of the barn behind the rectory. Instead of using a wheel, he crossed two thin slivers of wood cut from a roof shingle. These he fastened together at right angles to each other, like the blades of a windmill. Then he covered them with a paste he made of flour and water. He joined the "wheel" by silk thread to a pulley and a pencil. One of the On Furstenburg boys came to watch, drawn to the scene by the sounds in the barn, but Nikki was so intent upon his work that he was completely unaware of the other boy, who watched in silent fascination as Nikki painstakingly removed the bugs from the jar, one at a time, and glued their feet to the surface of the crossed blades—four bugs to each half of each blade— sixteen bugs in all. Then he stood up to watch eagerly for the result of his experiment. He was proud and excited when the frenzied whirring of wings as the bugs struggled to free themselves from the paste caused the crossed pieces to turn laterally. Elatedly he watched as the slack in the thread was taken up and the pencil began to turn. And then he realized that he had an audience.

"It works! It works!" he cried. "Of course it doesn't turn fast enough, but that's easy. All I have to do is add more bugs. Stay here and don't touch it. Don't let anything happen to it! I'm going to get Mother."

When Mrs. Tesla saw her son's flushed cheeks and shining eyes, her first thought was that he had a fever. She ran to him in alarm.

"Come with me. Mama," he cried. "You must. I've invented a motor. It will turn your eggbeater!"

Laughing in relief, she allowed herself to be pulled out of the kitchen toward the barn. But she did not laugh as she watched the rapidly fluttering wings of the imprisoned bugs propelling the little "motor." For the first time Nikki, staring up at her anxiously, saw on her face the look he had often seen there when she had been listening to one of Dane's intelligent observations, and Nikki knew that his efforts had at last been rewarded.

"It hasn't got enough power yet," his mother said seriously, "but it's wonderful, Nikki—really wonderful."

The two of them and little Alfred con Furstenburg stood gazing at the miniature contraption tor several seconds before Mrs. Tesla spoke again: "Don't you think it's cruel, Nikki?"

"Cruel!" he exclaimed indignantly. "Why? Bugs are of no use. This makes them useful! Don't you see. Mama? All I have to do is add four more bugs to each crosspiece and it will turn the upright fast enough to beat your eggs. I've got plenty of bugs. They're right here in this—"

Nikki stopped abruptly and gazed in shocked surprise at the empty jar he had taken from the shelf below the work table.

"That's funny," he said, "they were right here in this jar."

Slowly he turned toward the uninvited guest. The smallest of the On Filibustering tribe grinned and patted his stomach. Without a moment's hesitation Mrs. Tesla grabbed the young man by the nearest available appendage—which happened to be his ear—and hurried him into the house where certain crude but effective remedies were quickly applied. Shortly thereafter, looking a little green, he was sent home and Mrs. Tesla made it very clear to Nikola that he was to discontinue "Operation Eggbeater" as of that moment. Nikola didn't feel too badly. He had succeeded in inventing and operating a sixteenth motor—which was something his brother Dane had never done—and he had the pleasure of beholding that very special look on his mother's face.

When he was ten, Nikola entered the Real Gymnasium of Go spic. This four year institution was similar to an American grammar and junior high school, and served to introduce Nikola to more advanced studies. He particularly enjoyed mathematics; and the memory training received at home, plus a natural liking for the subject, sent him rocketing to the head of the class, which did not increase his popularity with his fellow students. When Nikki first demonstrated his amazing ability to supply formulas and solve equations with lighting speed, even his teachers were amazed, and it took very little prompting from the On Filibustering boys to make the entire faculty suspicious. Nikki was accused of cheating and the Countess con Filibustering demanded that he be expelled from school.

One day the Reverend Tesla asked Nikki to come into his study. "Have you been cheating, Nikola?" he asked.

"No, Papa."

"That's what I told Mr. Oberndorf, the principal. He says that you answer the questions more rapidly than any ten year old boy could possibly work out the answers. He believes that you see the questions before class, or that you have obtained a book with answers in it. He doesn't quite know, you see, but he is sure there is something wrong."

"I haven't cheated."

The Reverend Tesla looked at his son and smiled. "Tell me Nikki, are you doing what you used to do at home—I mean in Smiljan?"

Nikki grinned and nodded. "I picture in my mind the formula or the equation," he said. "It's as if I saw it written and then worked out on a blackboard. It doesn't take me very long to work it out when I can see it that way."

"And you can always see it? Your memory, or whatever it is, never fails you?"

"No, papa."

"Then we will request a test in the classroom, before witnesses, with problems that are made up on the spot! Come, let us go to the school. I think I'm going to enjoy this."

Nikki passed with ease every test that was put to him, but he was not elated. In such an atmosphere of distrust and enmity he was unhappy and lost.

"Father, may I go to a Higher Real Gymnasium when I finish here?" Nikki asked. "I think I can find a way to earn a living if I have four years in a first class Higher Gymnasium."

"The tuition is very high, Nikola," the Reverend Tesla answered, "but I'll see what I can do when the time comes."

"Perhaps if I could get a job," Nikki suggested, "I could begin to earn part of the expenses."

The Reverend Tesla smiled. "It hasn't come to that yet, Nikki," he answered. "And I don't want you overworking yourself. You're not too strong and—"

"I'd love to get a job. Father. I won't work too hard, I promise."

But there were very few jobs open to young boys, and those that existed paid too little or required time that was needed for classes and homework, but Nikki's persistence in seeking work was rewarded by the discovery that there was at least one job in Go spic for which the supply of eligible applicants never seemed to equal the demand. Librarians and assistants were always needed in the town library as well as in the primary and high school libraries. When Nikki inquired further into this possibility, he discovered why there always seemed to be vacancies: a librarian—even a second assistant—was required to have enough working knowledge of German, French, and Italian to enable him to read book titles and have some idea of the contents of the books written in those languages.

The Real Gymnasium offered a class in German to its underclassmen, but French was taught only to juniors and seniors, and Italian not given at all. So Nikki set about teaching himself.

Mrs. Tesla spoke all three languages fluently, relying solely on her memory of the sound of the spoken words. Nevertheless, by asking her the meaning of words, Nikki used his ability to visualize, so that he could create a definite picture in his mind of the way the spoken word would look on paper. Also, there were books in all three languages in his father's library and he took one to bed with him every night.

Fearing that Nikki would strain his eyes by doing so much reading in addition to his schoolwork, the Reverend Tesla urged the boy to ease the pressure he had imposed upon himself. But Nikki had not learned how to give sparingly of himself or his energy.

"If you're not careful, you'll have us all in the poorhouse," his father said teasingly. "Ten or twelve whole candles every single week!"

Oversensitive about being a financial burden to his parents, Nikola did not realize that his father was only speaking for his own good, to persuade him to use his eyes more carefully. That afternoon the boy went out to the town dump and found a large piece of tin. He brought it home and in the cellar he bent and hammered it into a candle mold that would make several candles at a time. Next, he went from room to room collecting all the candlesticks and candle holders, and diligently scraped the melted wax from their sides and bases. Then he went out into the back yard and built a little fire of twigs and dead leaves and melted the hardened wax scrapings. A ball of string that he had been carrying around in his pocket for weeks—for no particular reason except that he felt he'd find a use for it someday—now served to furnish him with wicks. Holding a piece of string into the mold with one hand, he poured in the melted wax with the other, hid the filled mold under a bush, and left it to harden. After a hurried supper, during which he was twice accused of gobbling his food, he rushed outdoors to discover himself the proud owner of eight perfectly formed candles.

For the next few days Nikola lived in hopes that his father would again bring up the matter of his extravagance so that he could have the pleasure of explaining that these particular candles were costing the family nothing. But with the perversity that Nikki felt adults so often displayed, the Reverend Tesla made no further comment on his son's reading habits. So the boy continued to read for long hours every night. Even so, progress seemed painfully slow to him, for his mind was always racing ahead to the finished job.

Progress with his other major project was also painfully slow at this time. In competing with the "genius" of Dane, he felt that he should fully understand what the word itself meant. The definition in the dictionary didn't tell him very much, so he began to study the biographies of men who had been acclaimed geniuses. Still, he had no very clear idea of what made them members of that select society. All he could discover was that most geniuses behaved differently—went barefoot or dressed oddly, or were "absentminded." One fact, however, stood out. Practically none of them was called a genius while alive, and Nikki could not help wondering if he, too, would have to die before he would be recognized as a genius. There would be no satisfaction in that! He wanted to be around when his family and neighbors exclaimed over his great achievements and success.

He came to the conclusion at last that a genius was someone who did something that no one had done, or thought of doing, before; and he determined that he would think of something— the sooner the better. Then, just a day or two after he had reached this decision, he happened to pass a group of boys practicing archery. He stopped to watch and was surprised to note how short the trajectory of the arrows was. The boys seemed to use a great deal of effort and muscle in pulling back the bowstring. And yet when released, the arrows flew in an almost straight line toward the target some fifty yards away.

He asked to be allowed to try a shot. Permission granted, he drew the bowstring taut and released the arrow. Everyone was amazed to see how true his aim was, but he was not at all impressed with his own performance. There was no real sense of release—no feeling of unleashed power. He imagined himself the arrow, and was disappointed because he felt as if he were wobbling slowly through the air instead of sailing through ?it cutting it cleanly and sharply, the way a diver, in performing a swan dive, seems to cleave the air like a knife edge.

He went home and cut himself a length of ash from a little tree behind the rectory. He whittled it to the right thickness and shaped the grip to fit his right hand, for he was left handed. After it was carved and molded and sanded, he held it over a great iron kettle filled with boiling water.

How he happened to think of doing this he did not know, but he felt certain that steaming the wood would leave it more flexible and thus allow him to shape it more readily. He felt that part of the power of the bow was lost in the width of the single arc and that if the ends of the bow could be straight, with the curve only in the center section, the force of the bow, hence the velocity of the arrow, could be greatly increased.

His very first attempt confirmed both theories. The heated wood bent easily under pressure and when it cooled it hardened into a bow resembling a "cupid's mouth" instead of the single arc bow used by the other boys. The bowstring could be pulled back further, and when he tried it he was delighted to learn that he had made a bow with about five times the propelling power of the bow he had handled that morning.

But he was still far from satisfied. He knew that there must be some way of drawing the bowstring tighter. And, just as he had always been able to visualize a problem in geometry or algebra, now there came into his mind a picture of a bow that could shoot farther and harder than the one he had made. It was not exactly a picture that came into his mind; it was more like a three dimensional image. He had never seen a picture of a crossbow. He had never even heard of an arrestable. And yet he was able to think of and make a bow that rested on a crossbeam with the bow in horizontal instead of vertical position. The bowstring was pulled taut by a hand screw, much like the pegs on a violin which, when turned, tighten the strings to the desired pitch. A small wooden trigger, very much like the latch on the Teslas' front door, released the tightened string and sent the arrow speeding through the air with such velocity that it sailed for as much as five hundred yards. At the short range of eight feet the arrow was thrust forward with such tremendous force that it would completely penetrate a plank an inch thick.

Shooting with a crossbow, Nikki so far outclassed his rivals that the fun soon went out of competition. Then, suddenly, everyone wanted one of "Nikki's crossbows," as they were called. Nikki sold arbalests as fast as he could turn them out, subsequently making a handsome profit. He hid the money in one of his mother's discarded stockings in the bottom drawer of his bureau. It was actually his first marketable invention. He had learned that there were other ways of making money than by having a job.

Encouraged by his sale of the arrestable and thrilled by the feeling of excitement and elation that he always got from watching an arrow in flight, he decided that he would attempt to make a flying machine. He had just learned in school about a vacuum—the space within a container from which all air has been exhausted. He had learned that every object on the earth is subject to normal atmospheric pressure of approximately fourteen pounds per square inch of surface, but that objects in a vacuum are free of such pressure. He decided that the pressure of fourteen pounds would be enough to rotate a cylinder at high speed. A completed picture came into his mind: he would build an airtight box around half of a cylinder and have the other half exposed to air pressure. In his mind's eye he could see the cylinder attached to a propeller that was turning so fast it was just a gleam in the sunlight and he, Nikki, with his vacuum box strapped to his back, was being propelled through the air in the winged flight of one of his own arrows. He had no way of knowing, of course, that his youthful theory was incorrect and would not work. There were no courses in manual training at the Real Gymnasium, no shop work of any kind, so Nikki had to borrow tools and figure out his own methods of construction. It took many weeks to build a wooden box and fit a cylinder into one end of it so precisely that there would be no air leakage, and during this time he cheered himself on with the thought that, if he succeeded, he would be performing two feats at once. He would be hailed as a genius and he would make a lot of money—enough to pay tuition at the Higher Gymnasium. And, best of all, he would fly!

When the cylinder and box were finished, he transformed an everyday air pump, which he borrowed from a livery stable in Go spic, into a vacuum pump by reversing the valves. Then he attached the pump to the box. Discovering that the cylinder revolved only so long as a vacuum remained, he realized at once that the box was not airtight and he would have to keep pumping all the time and this would not allow him much freedom to fly!

He was disappointed but he had learned that vacuum power could be used. He believed that someday he would find something to which he could apply this newly discovered source of power. Meanwhile he would go back to the study of languages so that he could get a job in the library. It wouldn't pay as much, or as quickly, as an invention might, but it would be safer and surer.

The failure of his flying machine convinced him that he was not a natural born genius. With this admission came the beginning of an idea so big, so staggering, that he became hypnotized by its limitless possibilities. The idea as it headfirst occurred to him was a simple one: he wondered whether a person could make a genius of himself. It was as simple and unpretentious as that. Some people dieted to lose weight, and others ate lots of bread and potatoes to get fatter. Could a person select certain emotions and feelings and discard others so that his thinking would be unbiased by love or affection or personal prejudice? The more he thought about it, the more the idea appealed to him. If he could only make himself into a sort of synthetic genius—a superman—he believed that his parents would be envied by parents all over the world. But he didn't know where or how to begin. He didn't know what should be cultivated and what discarded. He would have to study and think, and hope that with knowledge would come the answer.

He plunged into his studies with renewed energy, and by the time he had completed the course at the Gymnasium four years later he had won the reputation of being an excellent and serious scholar. He was graduated with honors, one of the top students in his class, and his mother and father told him they were very proud of him. They said so over and over— almost as if they were trying to convince themselves, he thought. Perhaps they were proud of him in the same way that they had been proud of Angelina and Milka when they had married, but not proud in the way they had been proud of Dane. There had been a light in their eyes, a tremor in their voices, which were not there now.

Nikola was given the hoped for job in the town library, and for a time all thoughts of supermen were erased from his mind. Great doors were opened wide and he was admitted into worlds he had never dreamed of: German literature, the works of French poets, scientific treatises from all over the world. He was amazed to learn how much more the scientists of Germany and Italy seemed to know than had been taught in the unthoughtful Real Gymnasium of Go spic

As he read volume after volume and catalogued them with meticulous care, he came to the amused conclusion that the only thing he had "invented" that nobody else had ever thought of seemed to be the underpowered motor 1

That summer of his fourteenth birthday he was content. The days were never long enough for him. He read incessantly, often taking the library books with him when he went for walks in the woods or lazed comfortably on the banks of a little stream near the outskirts of the city.

On one of these occasions he was sitting under a tree on a hilltop overlooking the countryside, with Keno snoring gently beside him. The sky was blue, the white church steeples were sharply outlined in the clearness of the pleasantly warm summer day. Deeply engrossed in his book, Nikola did not notice the sudden appearance of a fat gray cloud directly overhead. Suddenly he was startled by a brilliant lightning flash. Immediately following it came the rain.

Nikola sat with the book open on his knees, the rain beating unheeded against his face as he realized a connection between the two events. The lightning, then the rain. As if the cloud had been punctured like a paper bag, releasing its torrential contents. If this were so, he thought—if lightning caused the rain to fall—then man could control weather, tor man would one day be able to make lightning. On a tiny scale he had seen man made lightning in the physics laboratory when Professor Gruditsch had caused an electric spark to leap from one electric pole to its opposite. Nikola's conclusions were based on his observations and, as such were justified. However, further study would have shown him that the rain came first but took longer to reach the earth.

Nikola's first impulse was to cry aloud to all who would listen that he had made a great discovery—but in a moment he conquered the impulse. People would laugh or, even worse, would look at him pityingly as he had sometimes seen them looking at Poor Jon, the simpleminded country boy who often wandered the streets of Go spic. No. He would not talk of this idea. Not yet—perhaps not for a long time. He would wait until he had won the respectful attention of the scientific world. When everyone looked up to him and listened to his every word—that would be the moment. Just then Keno gave himself a mighty shake, splattering water from his shaggy coat all over Nikola and the library book he still held open and rain soaked on his lap.

CHAPTER 4

FOR WEEKS Mrs. Tesla and her husband had been worrying about their son. They knew he had his heart set in entering the Higher Real Gymnasium in Carlstadt that fall. The money for his tuition had been set aside, but they were troubled by the problem of living expenses so far away from home. Also, they were concerned for their son's health and the possibility of his becoming ill, with only total strangers to care for him. They both felt that Nikola was not too strong and that he drove himself too hard. When Mrs. Tesla remembered a distant cousin living in Carlstadt, they hoped that this might solve all of the difficulties.

"I'll write Cousin Sarah right now," the Reverend Tesla exclaimed and went into his study.

The response to that letter was everything that they had hoped for. Cousin Sarah and her husband, Colonel Brancovic, would be glad to have young Nikola live with them while he was attending the Higher Gymnasium. He must be sure to bring plenty of warm things to wear, for the winters in Carlstadt were often severe.

The weeks immediately preceding Nikki's scheduled departure afforded him ample opportunity to test his growing theory of renunciation and self-discipline The library job did not pay a salary, but Nikki would receive a fee upon the completion of the cataloguing. A great deal of work remained to be done. In order to finish the job and collect the fee he had to forget all about eye strain, nervous tension, fear of failure, and normal weariness and direct his thought and energies to the job at hand.

He completed the catalogue two days before he was to leave for Carlstadt. The Board of Trustees of the library told him over and over again how pleased they were, how grateful, and how impressed they were with the high quality of his work. He listened with ill-concealed impatience, waiting only to be paid so that he might hurry home and live in actuality a scene he had often visualized.

He was glad that his mother was out marketing. That was as he'd imagined. His father was in his study. That, too, was right. His spirits rose as he sneaked up the stairs, carefully avoiding the sixth step that always groaned and the eighth that squeaked. He hurried to his room and to the bureau drawer where he had for so long kept the stocking which served him as a bank. Here he had accumulated the money from whatever small jobs he had been able to achieve in the past four years, and the money he had made from the sale of the arbalests. He took the money he had just received and stuffed it into the stocking, smiling in anticipation of the look on his father's face, alight with happy surprise and pride—yes, at last—pride in his son's achievement.

Quickly, with hands that were so awkward they seemed to belong to someone else, he stuffed the paper money into the stocking, taking care that it rested on top and in no way muffled the comforting clinking of the heavy silver coins. Then he went downstairs, purposely treading heavily, and knocked loudly, imperiously. He smiled, knowing exactly what he was going to say. "Father," he would say, "I bring you this money with a request for your forgiveness for the trouble and worry I—"

The door opened and his father stood in the doorway just as Nikki had known he would—smilingly but with his thoughts still far away, as they often were when he was interrupted while working on a sermon.

"Why, Nikki!" the Reverend Tesla exclaimed. "I didn't hear you come home! Come in, boy, and tell me what's on your mind."

This, too, was exactly right. Nikki had known he would say that—use those very words.

"What's this?" his father asked, looking down at the bulging black stocking dangling from Nikki's fist.

To his utter amazement Nikki heard himself speaking.

"Here. It's for you," he said and thrust the stocking awkwardly toward his father's chest. The Reverend Tesla accepted it wonderingly, looking at it vaguely as if he felt he should know what it was but didn't. Then he smiled.

"Why, it's your money, Nikola. The library paid promptly, I see . . . For me, you said?"

Suddenly all vagueness left him. He looked sharply at Nikola and then raised the stocking to better examine its contents.

"This is a great deal of money, Nikola. Much more than the library was to pay you. Why are you giving it to me?"

"I—I want you to have it," Nikki stammered. "It's for the dress—the dress I spoiled, the windows I broke, the candles I used—It's for—"

He stopped speaking. A look of such wonder had come to his father's face that he was frightened. He had never seen that look before and he didn't know what it meant. Suddenly he saw his father's eyes fill with tears as he dropped the stocking to the floor with a loud clank. Then the Reverend Tesla reached out and pulled his thin, tall son close to him.

"Nikki, Nikki, is that what it has been all this time? Is that the wall that came between us? Have you come home at last— now that you are going away?"

He pushed the boy away from him with a roughness that tried to mask his deep emotion. Then he tousled Nikki's long, dark hair and father and son grinned at each other. A bond, closer than any Nikki had ever known, was established between them. He felt warmth and happiness coursing through him.

"If you had only told us what you were thinking and doing," his father said. "After this, if you are troubled—"

"I'll tell you. Father. I promise."

"This money," the Reverend Tesla said, stopping to pick up the forgotten stocking, "this money we will set aside for any future education or a vacation or whatever else you wish. It's yours. Neither your mother nor I would want to spend money that you have earned. And, one more thing: I do not mean to preach a sermon to you, Nikola, but remember, your mother and I love you. Not matter what you might do—even if we were ashamed of you, of what you had done or failed to do—we would not stop loving you. That is what you must never forget."

"I'll remember," Nikola said.

Nikola remembered. He was remembering now as he sat in the grimy third class coach of the old fashioned wooden train that was taking him on the long journey to Carlstadt. He was remembering the warmth he had felt. He was remembering . . .

Clicker, clicker, CLACKCLACK, clicker

He had unfortunately been assigned to a seat over what he realized must be a flat wheel. The repeated break in rhythm was irritating. He wondered if he would be allowed to move to another seat or another coach. This was his first train ride and he didn't know.

Clicker, clicker, CLACKCLACK, clicker

He was very tired. His face felt hot. Leaning his cheek against the cool glass of the window, he looked out but saw nothing of the woods and streams that were flashing by. His thoughts were turned inward. He saw again the scene at the tavern in Go spic where the coach that made connections with the railroad stopped to change horses and take on passengers. He tried to close his mind to the annoyance of the train noises.

Clicker, clicker, CLACK, CLACK, clicker . . .

He was recreating scenes that had taken place the past two days—his room at home, Keno following him about from room to room, sensing something amiss, seemingly afraid to let his master out of sight. His mother's fingers flying as she performed last minute miracles on last year'& clothes, which were all much too small for him now . . . He had never ceased to wonder at his mother's dexterity—her fingers seemed large and clumsy looking

It had required very little teasing to have her stop what she was doing and laugh as she beckoned him closer. "All right, all right, you silly boob! I'll show you again that I can still do it. But, mind, this is the last time."

Then, while he had watched, fascinated, she had plucked a hair from one of his bushy eyebrows and proceeded, with lightning speed, to tie three knots in it. She had held it out to him.

"Here. Take it. Look at it. Are there three knots in it?"

"There are three knots in it."

"Satisfied?"

"Yes!"

Then they had both laughed and she had given him a little push.

"Now go away and let me finish altering this coat or your hands will hang down below the sleeves like a pair of hams in the smokehouse."

Nikola remembered his father, thinking up excuses that had brought him back from the church to the house. He saw himself, with his two new straw suitcases, walking through the little foyer toward the front door. His parents had preceded him and were waiting on the sidewalk, chatting with the driver of the hired Victoria He remembered turning back and seeing Keno at the foot of the stairs, not making any attempt to follow him, just standing there, quietly looking at him. . . .

Nikola opened his eyes and looked out the train window. He wanted to shut out of his mind the look of betrayal he had seen in the dog's eyes. Keno thought he was being deserted. Nikola had wanted desperately to drop his bags and run back, to put his arms around the big dog and explain. But if he did he knew he would cry and he mustn't do that.

"I'll be back, Keno," he had muttered. "I'll come back."

Then he had almost run out of the hall and pulled the front door shut with the back of his heel.

He'd have to put that out of his mind, he thought. It was all very well to promise to remember—but he must not do so. He would not be able to concentrate on his work if he were to go on remembering. For the time being, at least, he must forget Keno. He must forget Marica and Angelina and his brotherly, blubbering while they tried to comfort his mother. He must forget their tenderness and warmth . . .

A fine specimen of a superman he had turned out to be. He had allowed his feelings and emotions to crowd out more important things: his studies, the new courses, the library, awaiting him in Carlstadt. He felt as if he had lost ground which must now be made up. Family affection, the knowledge that he was loved, pleasant as they were, must not be allowed to come between him and his momentarily forgotten goal. It was not enough to have his father pleased with him just because he was a member of the Tesla family. That had not been of his own doing. That was nothing to be proud of or praised for. He must stop caring what people thought or felt about him. Suddenly he began to have a feeling of kinship with his dead brother Dane. For the first time he thought that perhaps Dane had deliberately refused to allow himself to be won over by Keno's affectionate nature; perhaps he had been right to think only of Trier's cleverness. Nikola promised himself he would be more wary in the future. If he were to become a self-trained genius he would have to avoid emotional entanglements. He was going to a place where he was completely unknown. He would start all over again—make a brand new beginning. He would not make the mistake of allowing himself to become fond of anyone. He would not make friends, for they might unwittingly make demands upon him. He would have no ties Ana he would stop thinking of the past. And he would work, work, work. Clicker, clicker, WORK' WORK.I clicker . . .

Circumstances helped to make it easy for him to keep his resolution.

Cousin Sarah and her husband, "the Colonel," were not the sort of people to appeal to Nikola. Sarah, tall, straight backed, and bucktoothed, had little natural warmth and absolutely no charm. The couple had no children and she liked the idea of having someone about the house to "make a fuss over"—as Nikola's mother would have said. She was a kindly person with the best of intentions but not one whit of understanding of a boy as reserved and withdrawn as Nikola chose to be.

The Colonel, on the other hand, was short and squat and always spoke as if he were bellowing orders to his battalion. He was no conversationalist and took not the slightest interest in science or anything that smacked at all of the intellectual. The only interest he could share with the shy boy who had suddenly become a member of his family was the flower garden in which he took an inordinate pride. And after a week of exclaiming over the amazing growth and variety of the petunias, Nikola felt that the subject had been pretty thoroughly ex exhausted

Perhaps Nikola might have been lonely had he permitted himself to contrast this dreary, arid home with the rich, warm, and colorful one he had left behind. But he stuck firmly to his resolution and thought only of the present and the future. The tact that his courses were difficult and required complete con concentration helped him to get through what might otherwise have been a difficult time.

He found that physics attracted him more than any other subject, for in this course the wonders of electricity were studied and discussed. The knowledge that there were units of electricity in the very air he breathed—that all living things were surrounded by it, that it was ever present as a source of limitless power that could be tapped by manmade mechanical contraptions—filled him with excitement. He longed for the day when he would understand it enough to permit clear, original thinking. He felt that it was something so miraculous that, once understood, it must change man's whole concept of life and death.

In his reading at the library he had come across books on electricity written by two well-known German scientists, both of whom mentioned the contemporary work of an American named Thomas Alva Edison. Nikola was not certain whether the German authors were fully explaining the work of this man or were merely giving their own appraisal of its value. He decided to add the study of the English language to his already crowded curriculum in order to read the American's own descriptions of his experiments. He found English much more difficult than German or French or Italian, and he spent most of his "free" time surrounded by lexicons and dictionaries while trying to decipher the abstruse technical explanations of the early experiments with electric light.

The first few weeks at college he found to be both stimulating and depressing. The more he read and studied, the more it seemed to him that man had made only a tiny dent in the vast and almost endless fields of knowledge. He was reminded of Keno digging furiously in the sandy soil of a little beach near his home in Smiljan. The dog had put every ounce of energy into his digging, yet the taster he dug, the more sand slid down the sides of the hole, so that a good proportion of the dog's energy was wasted in clearing away sand that had been scooped out several times before. And there was too little time, he thought, for wasted effort. He became more than ever convinced that his superman theory offered the only hope. If he could eliminate from his own life all distracting influences, he stood a chance of being able to accomplish something of real scientific value in the short period of one lifetime. But time was passing. There just weren't enough hours in the day.

Although they had never met, and would have had absolutely nothing in common had they done so, the dean of the Higher Gymnasium and Cousin Sarah agreed on one point: young Nikola Tesla was working too hard. Both of these individuals felt it their duty to take pen in hand . . .

The Reverend Milutin Tesla took off his glasses and sat quietly staring into space. He had just finished reading the two letters aloud to his wife.

"What can we do?" he asked after a moment. "He doesn't answer my letters. I don't even know that he reads them."

"If I had only learned to write!" Mrs. Tesla exclaimed.

Her husband smiled at her. "What could you write to him that I can't?"

"I'm his mother. I'd know what to say!"

"Well, I'm his father—and I don't!"

"Let's ask him to come home for the Christmas holidays. Once he's here we might be able to persuade him to overstay his vacation for at least a week or two."

"It's an idea, certainly," the Reverend Tesla agreed. "Well Worth a try."

CHAPTER 5

SITTING ON THE EDGE of his bed in his narrow little room at Cousin Sara's, Nikki finished reading his father's letter. He held it in his long, tapering fingers and stared unseeingly at the whitewashed wall, seeing instead his home at Christmastime . . .

the tree, the lighted candles, the gaily wrapped gifts, his sisters, nieces, nephews—the tolling church bell, the choir singing The Messiah—Keno walking on his hind legs begging for Christmas candy. The whole family would gather around the big round table in. the dining room—this occasion would call for the extra leaves on the table so that it would be oval instead of round—his father carving the Christmas goose.

At this point he interrupted his thinking. He must not think of such things! It made him remember how hungry he was. He wished Cousin Sarah would get over the silly idea that, just because he was thin, he had a small stomach and that overeating might distend it! Whenever she caught the Colonel trying to slide an extra piece of meat off the platter and onto Nikola's plate, she would embark on a ten minute lecture describing the dangers of overeating. The meat she had served that evening had been sliced paper thin and had been no more satisfying than the paper he was holding in his hand. No, he mustn't allow himself to think of Christmas dinner. It seemed to him that he was always hungry, and the thought of good food and plenty of it might prove to be the weak link in his armor.

In spite of the letter Nikola had no intention of going home for Christmas. This was the first real chance he had been given to test his new found theory. Families and gifts and loved ones were wonderful, and most people should enjoy and appreciate them; but scientists had no time to waste. If he stayed on at college for the holidays he would have the library and the physics laboratory to himself. He could afford the luxury of wasting a little time on working out new ideas without the interruption of classes and lectures. It could be a wonderful holiday and a productive one. He must not let himself think of a juicy roast goose, his mother's delicious stuffing. The rich pastries and glazed fruits . . .

"I WILL NOT GO HOME FOR CHRISTMAS!" he said aloud and with great determination. He had passed his first test.

Everything seemed to conspire to make Christmas Day in Carlstadt the most wonderful one Nikola had ever known.

First of all, it had begun to snow on Christmas Eve, and when he awakened early the next morning he saw that the whole countryside was completely blanketed. It looked so clean and inviting that, forgetting all about breakfast, he bundled up in heavy sweaters his mother had knitted for him, pulled on his warmest boots, and hurried out of the house.

The library being closed for the day, he decided to do his thinking and figuring while he walked toward a high mountain that, in the clear air, seemed a good deal closer than it actually was.

The campus was deserted. The common was a vast expanse of white, and he broke trail across it, glancing up at the huge gray masses of stone that were the college buildings. He paused to examine more closely the hulk of the Administration Building. It was of Gothic architecture, with great, leering gargoyles perched on each of the four cornices. Usually their crouching forms seemed misshapen and meaninglessly ugly to him, but today, crowned with cones of snow, their gaping mouths adorned with icicle beards, they seemed like merry, laughing clowns or dwarfs. Suddenly aware of the cold and, holding mittened hands over his ears, he turned and stamped on his way toward the mountain. Not a soul was in sight, not a sound broke the silence. What a perfect time for concentration! As he trudged onward, he began to work out the formulas he needed to calculate the stresses and strains of the gigantic trusses needed to support a unique transportation system that would encircle the globe.

This was Nikola's favorite game. He didn't really think the plan was feasible; but, as some people find pleasure and relaxation in playing solitaire, he found a guilty pleasure in daydreaming about this difficult and intriguing problem. His idea was to build a ring around the earth at the Equator—a rigid structure constructed on an enormous system of scaffolding,

Once the ring was complete, the scaffolding would be removed leaving the ring suspended in space, held there firmly by the constant pull of gravity and free to rotate at the same speed as the earth. If the ring could be made to stand still, the earth would spin within it at the rate of a thousand miles per hour, enabling a tourist to "travel" around the earth in a single day!

If he could only find, discover, or invent a reactionary force strong enough to counteract the pull of gravity and cause the ring to stand still!

He created and discarded formula after formula as he trudged through the heavy snow. The pealing of church bells recalled him to awareness of the world around him. He was halfway up the high mountain and the sun was nearly at its zenith. He paused to look down at the college and the city in the valley below him. The air was so clear that he could even distinguish the snowcapped gargoyles. He thought he could see wreathes in the windows of faculty houses surrounding the campus. He was sure that he could even see his own footprints marring the unbroken whiteness of the campus itself. Directly below him, at the base of the mountain, was a little cluster of small wooden houses from which sounds of laughter rose to remind him that it was Christmas. Suddenly he felt very small and lonely and homesick

Who was he, he asked himself, to think he could become a great scientist? What made him think he was destined to benefit all mankind? Didn't his father preach that God would punish those who tried to usurp His powers? A ring around the world indeed! He hadn't even succeeded in making an airtight vacuum box!

Idly, and without thinking what he was doing, he stooped and gathered up two handfuls of snow, which he molded and packed into a snowball. Then, seeing what he had done, he took aim and threw the snowball at a nearby tree—and missed. He couldn't even hit a tree with a snowball! Quickly, he made some more and this time had better luck. He noticed that the snow that had missed their mark rolled a short distance down the slope, gathering more snow and growing quite large before they stopped moving. He wondered how big one would get if it rolled all the way down the steep mountain. He decided to find out, but the first few snowballs fell apart after traveling about twenty feet. He tried again. This time the snowball did not fall apart but rolled into a bramble bush. Idly he told himself to try just once more before returning home. The exercise had warmed him up, but it had also made him aware that he was hungry. He packed and pounded the snowball in his hands and then threw it underhand as if it were a bowling ball.

This time it rolled exactly as he wanted it to. As it gathered speed, it grew in a matter of seconds into a huge ball, reminding Nikola of a giant snowman. And it continued to grow as it plunged on down the side of the mountain. Then, due to its speed and the force of its headlong plunge, it dislodged a large rock, which crashed and bumped down the wooded slope ahead of it. The two flying missiles seemed to devour everything they encountered, and soon, before Nikola's horrified eyes, the whole mountainside seemed to be sliding and crashing down onto the group of little houses below him. Carrying trees and rocks and boulders with it, the heaving mass cut a swathe down the side of the mountain that left it looking as if a straight razor had been stroked through heavy shaving lather.

The avalanche was headed straight for the houses! Everyone inside would be crushed under that prodigious weight; the voices he had heard—the laughter—would be stilled forever. There was nothing he could do. He could not even scream a warning, for the noise of the avalanche—the sound of uprooted trees and clattering rocks—.would drown out his cries. He hoped that the sound itself would be a warning, but no one was running out of the houses.

And then came the miracle. From where he stood, Nikola could not tell exactly what happened. Somehow, that sliding, flowing, writhing mass was deflected and the avalanche suddenly changed its course and veered off at an angle.

Nikola felt a tremor through his thick soled boots as the mass harmlessly crashed to a halt in an empty field. Now he saw people running out of their houses and dropping to their knees in the snow, offering up thanks for their deliverance from catastrophe. He stepped back from the edge of the cliff—suppose someone should see and connect him with the avalanche! Deeply shaken, he sank down on a fallen log and dropped his head into his cupped hands.

Was this a warning to him, he wondered? Should he take it as a sign that he was trespassing in a realm reserved for a greater power and authority? He decided against this. He was only Nikola Tesla, a boy who had thrown a snowball and who was hardly important enough to attract the attention of any unearthly power. That crushing, roaring mass of destruction had been started by a snowball—a snowball the size of his fist— with snow he had held in the palm of one hand! The snowball had released the avalanche.

And suddenly he saw and understood something quite clearly. The snowball had triggered the avalanche in just the same way the trigger on his crossbow had released an arrow with the tremendous force that enabled it to pierce a one inch plank. The trigger did not have to be big or strong or in itself powerful. It simply had to release the powers of nature that surrounded it. It came to him in a flash as brilliant as any lightning flash that he, Nikola Tesla, could be a trigger. He would learn how to harness or unleash the power of the avalanche, the waterfall, rain, lightning! He would learn how to make dynamos and motors so that men might only have to throw a switch to release the power of a hundred galloping horses! He would learn how to make a water wheel that would generate enough electrical power to light up a whole city! He would learn to be an electrical engineer!

He stood up and took a deep breath. Suddenly he felt faint and dizzy. He had had a shock and he had seen a vision, but he realized that neither phenomenon was responsible for this feeling of lightheartedness. He had had nothing to eat since the night before and he was hungry!

He began the descent of the mountain, going out of his way to avoid being seen by the little crowd that had gathered to gaze awestruck at the hill that had been deposited in their midst. It was nearly two in the afternoon when he reached home and there was a distinct air of hauteur about Cousin Sarah when she opened the door for him.

"Well, Nikola, I'm pleased to see that you've decided to honor us with your company for a late Christmas dinner."

The accent on the word "late" was taint but unmistakable— as was the aroma of cooking that wafted out from the kitchen.

"Merry Christmas, my boy," the Colonel boomed, coming into the hallway. "Did Cousin Sarah tell you about the surprise?"

Nikola shook his head.

"Your mother has sent us a whole goose—all cooked and spiced, with slices of roasted orange—"

"It almost seems as if your mother thought me incapable of cooking a goose well enough to please you, Nikola. I s'pose I really ought to be hurt."

"There are two kinds of dressing, Nikki," the Colonel interrupted. "Oyster and chestnut. Fairly makes your mouth water"

"There's a letter of instructions with it from your father, Nikola. He writes that you're to be given a drumstick, a wing, and four thick slices of breast meat It will probably make you ill, but since—"

"Merry Christmas, Cousin Sarah!" Nikki cried and, throwing both his long arms around her bony shoulders, whirled her out of the hall toward the kitchen.

Nikki was fourteen. He had discovered what he wanted to do with his life. And there was roast goose and all the trimmings for Christmas dinner!

CHAPTER 6

IN FEBRUARY, shortly before the midterm semester was scheduled to end, Nikola received another urgent plea from his father to come home. Keno was getting old and feeble, the letter said. He seemed to be lackadaisical and without the will to live. Perhaps if he were to see Nikki again . . . but, of course, dogs did grow old and one must get used to the idea of losing them one day . . .

This was another test, Nikki thought. A test much more difficult than any he had had to face so far. He remembered only too clearly the look of betrayal in the big dog's eyes. He also recalled his promise to return.

The fact that he was homesick made his decision more difficult. He missed his parents, his sister Marica. He wanted to feel Keno's heavy fur under his fingers. He longed to feel his mother's arms around him, see his father's lopsided smile. But he thought these longings were a sign of weakness. He believed with his whole mind that a scientist—a searcher after scientific truth—must live in a human vacuum in order to devote his whole self to his work. He believed that, just as members of a track team renounced alcohol and smoking in order to build their bodies up to the highest possible pitch of efficiency, so a scientist must renounce love and sentiment and friendship. He had managed to do without them for more than six months. If he weakened now he might never be able to develop immunity to them.

Reluctantly and painfully he wrote his father that he was behind in his studies and needed to stay in Carlstadt if he had any hope of catching up. Even as he wrote, he seemed to see die big dog sitting across the room from him, gazing at him with unwinking, reproachful eyes, but he forced himself to finish the letter.

"Ask Mother to try feeding Keno raw meat instead of the cooked table scraps. The raw meat might possibly give him back his strength. Don't worry about me. I'm feeling fine. Love, Nikki."

It was late in May when his father wrote to tell him that Keno had died. By that time Nikola had so steeled himself against the shock of the expected news that he was able to shut it out of his mind and concentrate on the coming examinations. He felt that, if he had been remiss or unfeeling, the only thing that would justify his action was success. He owed it to everyone who loved him to reach the highest pinnacle of fame. He knew now that he wished to become an engineer. If he could manage to pass its stiff exams and get into the Polytechnic Institute in Gratz, Austria . . .

He did not go home until the summer vacation. He had passed every test and examination that had been given him and, more than that, he had passed the tests he had imposed upon himself. He had made application for admission to the Polytechnic Institute only to be informed that applications from minors were not considered without the signature of at least one parent. He rebelled against his extreme youth but there was nothing to do except to ask his father's help. Since he had no confidence in his own ability to put this strongly and appealingly in a letter, he agreed at long last to heed the pleas of his parents and spend at least part of the summer vacation at home.

As he had feared, his father flatly refused to help him. "Nikki! Don't you ever look at yourself in the mirror?" he exclaimed. "Don't you realize that you are pale and gaunt? You look as if you were ready to drop at any moment. You can't go on like this. Your mother and I lived through the grief of losing one brilliant son. Don't ask us to do it again."

"But, Father . . ."

"It's no use, Nikki. I won't sign the application, I'd feel as if I were signing your death warrant."

Nikki said nothing and the two sat in silence for a long moment, before the Reverend Tesla spoke again:

"There's another thing, Nikki. Something I think you've forced out of your mind because you don't want to remember it."

"You mean because I haven't been home before and . . ."

His father looked at him sharply and Nikki knew that he had revealed more of his inner conflict than he had intended to.

"No, I wasn't thinking of Keno," he replied. "I was thinking of the army."

"The army!"

"You had forgotten, hadn't you? But you know that every boy in Gospic must serve three years in the army or go to jail."

"But that's impossible, Father! I can't take the time away from my work. Why, it would mean—three years! I can go through Polytechnic in that length of time! Isn't there anything we can do? Someone to see who might—"

"The Military Police paid me a visit only two weeks ago. They were very polite, very—genial, almost—they said that they just wanted to remind me that the army was looking forward to obtaining the services of my gifted son... next year. And they reminded me, gently and pleasantly, that the only admissible reason for failing to register is death or a critical illness. They would surely say that if you're well enough to apply for admission to Polytechnic, you're not too ill to serve in the army."

"Is there nothing we can do? Isn't Cousin George a colonel or a general or something?"

"Lieutenant Colonel, I believe. Oh yes, I've got high ranking relatives in the army. Even a brother—Uncle Alfred, whom you've never met—but I'm afraid they'd not be inclined to lend a sympathetic ear to any plea from me. No. No hope there. There is one way though."

"What is it? I'd do almost anything——"

"You might consider entering the church."

"The church! Oh no!"

"Your horror is not very flattering, Nikki."

"I'm sorry. I've never been able to understand how someone I—I respect as I do you—how you could have chosen the church as ... I've never been able to talk about it. I can't now."

"I got into the church in exactly the way I'm suggesting that you do, and for the same reason."

Nikola stared at his father as if he were seeing him for the first time. "You mean you didn't want to serve in the army, either? That you—"

The Reverend Tesla nodded, smiling a little at his son's amazement. "Ours is an old army family, Nikki," he said. "My great-great-grandfather was a general; my grandfather was too. My father was a colonel, and was up for promotion when he died. So you see, when I said I didn't believe in war as a means of settling a dispute between nations, I did not make myself very popular in my family. That's why those members of it who are still alive would not be very likely to help me keep my son from serving. I wanted to study medicine. I felt that there was a need in the world that I could fill. My father forced me to enroll in the Letz Military Academy. I stuck it out for nearly a year, but I could not stand the lack of privacy, the total disappearance of the individual ... the training of boys to be killers."

"So you——"

"It wasn't what you're thinking, Nikola." The Reverend Tesla smiled again as he saw the growing look of disapproval on his son's face. "You must believe me. It wasn't that way at all. I never pretended that I heard the 'call.' I never pretended to be a learned theologian. I told the chaplain at the school how a felt, and asked him if the church could use a man like myself—a man who loved people and whom people might learn to trust. I told him how little I knew and that I wasn't even certain what I believed."

Nikola relaxed. The frown left his face. His father, watching him anxiously, sat further back in his heavily carved chair and waited.

"I'm—I'm awfully glad you told me. Father," Nikola said at last. "It explains so many things. And you are good at it, and the parishioners do trust you and look to you for help in times of need. But I can't do it, Father. I would be doing it just to avoid the army and I can't do that. I don't believe in—in the sort of thing you believe in. And so it would be dishonest for me to pretend ..."

The Reverend Tesla sighed. "Of course you couldn't, Nikola," he said. "And I wouldn't want you to even if you could. I had hoped that you might bring yourself to discuss my beliefs and see whether they are too far apart to—"

"I know they are, Father!" Nikola exclaimed. "For one thing, you've often said you love people. I don't. It is mankind that I love."

"Aren't you—might not there be some who'd say that to take such an attitude is to play God? Only He has the right to judge people. Furthermore, my son, isn't mankind made up of people?" His father watched him searchingly.

"I s'pose it is. But in working out an invention that will benefit mankind, one does not think of helping any special kind of person—but the world as a whole."

"I see." At those words, Nikola looked up quickly to see if his father was laughing at him, but the Reverend Tesla's face was grave. Encouraged by his father's attentive listening, Nikola continued:

"The most important thing, though, is faith. You say that people in the church must have faith—in something, mustn't they?"

"There's no denying that,"

"Well, a scientist must not have faith in anything until it's proven. If a scientist sets out to prove a theory just because he has faith in it, he's likely to unconsciously twist the results to fit his theory or interpret them in a way not justified by the facts. And that's dishonest."

The Reverend Tesla leaned forward in his chair. "Nikola," he said with grave earnestness, "will you answer one question?"

"I'll try."

"What is it that a scientist is seeking?"

"Truth, Nikola told him.

His father asked, "His opinion of what truth is?"

"No! Truth—absolute truth."

"Have I your permission to ask another question?"

Nikki grinned and nodded.

"How does he know there is an absolute truth."

"He knows there is. He believes . . ."

Nikki stopped and stared at his father in such ludicrous amazement that his father could not help laughing.

"Of course. He believes, Nikki," he said. "We poor humans all believe in something or we couldn't go on. I won't ask any more questions. And believe me, I wasn't trying to trap you into agreeing with me, but I'm asking you please, my boy, please give it some thought, some serious thought. It offers the only way out of your dilemma—that is, if you could do it honestly."

"I will think about it. Father. I promise. But . . ."

"One more thing to think about," his father persisted. "Isn't it possible that what the scientist calls 'absolute truth,' others might call 'God'? Don't answer that now. Think about it. And now let's go in and ask your mother how supper's coming along."

Shortly after his return, Nikola overheard some boys discussing a classmate who was trying to attain leadership of the class,

"Who does he think he is?" one boy asked his companion. "Napoleon Bonaparte? The Man of Destiny?"

"Alexander the Great, probably," the other answered. "He wants to conquer the whole world."

Nikola could not help but wonder what they would say of him if they had the slightest inkling of the goal he had set for himself! An empire? The world? These were not for Nikki Tesla. He wanted to control the elements of nature, tame the universe and hand it over to the world for the benefit of mankind! They would almost certainly say he was crazy.

Perhaps they would say, as his father had hinted, that he was trying to play God.

But it wasn't as if he felt himself to be a Man of Destiny. Nor did he think for one instant that he had any Godlike power. If he had, he could have sat back on his lean haunches and waited for Fate to present him with the great invention, the discovery that would make him the benefactor of mankind, meanwhile basking in the warmth of his parents' love. He didn't feel that way at all. On the contrary, he felt completely inadequate for the task he had set himself unless he worked with a sort of desperate concentration on perfecting his ability to memorize and visualize so that he would achieve the highest possible sensitivity. Then, perhaps, the unseen mysteries of nature would fall into place, enabling him to unlock and release them in all their tremendous power.

He pursued his studies with even greater intensity and con concentration By now he was certain .that he could complete the four year course in three years, and he disciplined himself to ignore the high spirited activities of his classmates, and the repeated urgings of his parents to come for holiday visits, in order to devote his whole time and attention to the subjects required for his diploma.

As graduation time approached, the twin specters—the army and the church—were ever present, lurking in the back of his mind. He thought that perhaps his father had this problem in view when he again wrote that Nikola should not come home, but go away to some unfamiliar place to relax and be lazy. The more he examined this thought, however, the more he believed that there must be some other reason. It was not like his father to urge him to avoid facing an issue bravely and courageously. The Reverend Tesla would not suggest to his son that he run away.

In the midst of studying hard for final exams, the letter from home kept intruding into Nikola's thoughts. Had he offended his father? Was his mother ill? Were they trying to spare his feelings about something? He was about to graduate—completing a difficult course in three years' time—he was being graduated with honors at the age of seventeen. He wanted to return to Go spic and surprise his family with the news of his achievement. . . and apparently they did not want him to come home!

Nikola decided to wheedle information out of the Colonel. It was useless, he knew, to try to extract any secrets from his tight lipped Cousin Sarah, but the Colonel should be easy. One had only to ask him a few questions about "the old days," when he was a dashing lieutenant or a gallant captain in order to open the floodgates of that uncomplicated mind and let whatever small facts or secrets it might hold pour forth.

And it actually proved as easy as Nikola had supposed it would be. On the very first attempt he learned why his father did not want him to come home: Gospic was suffering the ravages of cholera. The dread disease, which was usually fatal, had taken a heavy toll of the population.

"You'd think that the doctors with all their talk and their pills and leeches, would be able to find some cure. But they haven't. It's still listed as a critical disease."

Nikola—whose thoughts had been far away as he wondered about his parents' health, moved by their desire to spare him the risk that they were facing daily—was suddenly alerted by the Colonel's words.

"Critical disease"? Hadn't his father said that the only excuse acceptable to the military authorities for exemption from three years' compulsory service was a critical illness? Perhaps he was being offered a way out! But did he have the courage to grasp the opportunity, considering the hazard involved?

As usual, when faced with the task of solving a difficult problem, Nikola felt the urgent need to be alone. He was not aware of leaving the room, or of passing men and women on the street, or of being hailed by classmates. He was trying to think things out ... trying to weigh the alternative clearly and with an open mind.

First he considered the army and what it would mean to enter the service. Three years of "Squads Right!" "Squads Left!" "Shoulder Arms!"—three years of being bellowed at by men like Colonel Brancovic, three years of learning how to follow orders without question and without thinking—three years in which to be trained not to think! To Nikola this seemed like a stupid and wicked waste of all the time and money and self-discipline that had gone into his education thus far. And waste of any kind was wrong.

The church? He felt that here, too, he would have to "unlearn" everything he had worked so hard to acquire. He meant no disparagement to those who labored for the spiritual wellbeing of their neighbors. He simply felt that he was not equipped for that work—and never could be. He had never been able to interest himself in people's everyday problems. He felt, with complete certainty, that no one would find comfort or relief by unburdening himself to his not sufficiently sympathetic ears. Nor would he ever have the strong faith that would be demanded of him. He was not at all certain that he believed in the existence of a God. How then, could he convince others?

At that point he allowed his thoughts to turn to where he felt they belonged. Electricity! The very word made his nerves tingle. Electricity! The almost miraculous force that scientists knew about but could not control. He felt as if electricity were a prisoner of stupidity and ignorance and there it was waiting for him to come along and release it. People were afraid to use it. There was not a house in any village or town or city in which there was one room lighted by electricity; they used candles and oil lamps and even gas. People were indeed afraid of it. To most of them the thunderbolt was still the symbol of an angry God. Stories about persons who had been badly "shocked" or severely burned by an electric current were repeated over and over. It reminded Nikola of the way people had reacted to a tiger he had once seen in Smiljan.

It had happened when he was a little boy. One of his father's rich parishioners had returned from a hunting trip in India. He had brought back with him a live Bengal tiger, which he planned to present to the zoo in Prague. For two days the magnificent animal had remained in its great wooden cage at the coach terminus at Smiljan, awaiting transportation. The cage was made of heavy troubadour planks, the corners and joints reinforced by iron plates. One side was open and closely barred. The big crate was all of ten feet square. Nikki had stood for hours, watching the great beast crouch and leap, fall back and leap again. The other onlookers had screamed with pleasurable horror at the thought that the beast might succeed in crashing its way to freedom; but Nikki had watched with wonder the tremendous beauty and power of those rippling muscles, the long, graceful, hurtling body, and he had thought over and over again: "Oh, if I could only muzzle and harness it! If I could harness it to a chariot, we could leap over the rooftops! We could travel faster than ten horses!"

He knew now that no one could have harnessed that animal; no one could have put all that partially revealed power to any useful purpose. But this was not true of electric power. It could be tamed; it could be harnessed. And he knew that he was capable of doing both. He would rather be dead than be deprived of the chance to try.

He made his decision. The day after graduation, he bade farewell to Cousin Sarah and the Colonel and left immediately for Go spic Confident in his ability to force his body to obey the dictates of his mind, he deliberately exposed himself to cholera. A week after his homecoming he was in a coma.

For the second time doctors visited the home of the Teslas. For the second time sympathetic neighbors said in lowered voices how dreadful it would be if the Teslas lost their brilliant son who was well on the way to becoming a genius.

Numb with fear and grief, Mrs. Tesla and her husband hovered by the bedside, wanting to be present if their son should return to consciousness. Nikola became weaker. He lost many pounds, which he could ill afford. The high cheekbones and long, thin nose seemed to be formed of wax instead of skin and bone. The boy often muttered in his restless sleep, but what he said meant nothing to his grieving parents. The doctors offered little hope.

"You must lie down. Mother," the Reverend Tesla said to his weeping wife. "You must rest or you'll get sick yourself. I'm not strong enough to face this alone. For my sake, rest. I'll stay with our boy."

For a long time the Reverend Tesla sat by his son's bedside, with a feeling of complete helplessness. He could almost sense the withdrawal of the boy's spirit as he lay there with his eyes closed, his black lashes emphasizing the pallor of his cheeks. All his prayers seemed to have been in vain. He leaned closer to hear what Nikola was saying:

"The tiger." The words came over and over again. "The tiger in the box."

To the father it sounded like meaningless delirium.

"They won't let me try to manage—tiger," Nikki murmured. "Won't—even—let me—try."

Almost roughly the harassed father slid his arm under the thin shoulders and turned the unconscious, unresisting body around to face him.

"Listen to me, Nikki," the Reverend Tesla said in a hoarse voice. "You've got to listen to me. You mustn't go away, Nikki. Wherever you are, listen to me. We want you to come back."

Nikola's eyes remained closed. His lips continued to move, forming words that were now soundless.

"Nikki, listen to me," his father repeated. "You won't have to go into the army—just come back to us. Come back, Nikki. I won't ever again ask you to follow in my footsteps. You can be an engineer, if that's what your heart is set on. Just come back."

Nikola sighed. The lips stopped moving. For one long moment the Reverend Tesla thought his son had died in his arms. Then slowly the long eyelashes quivered. Nikola opened his eyes and the Reverend Tesla saw that they were clear seeing and not feverish. And Nikki smiled.

"Thank you. Father," he said weakly. "You won't be sorry. You'll be proud of me. I'm going to be the best—the best engineer in the world."

CHAPTER 7

THE CRISIS ONCE PAST, Nikola recovered with a speed and resiliency that astounded both his parents and the attending physicians. They had prophesied that, if he recovered at all, it would take him many months to regain his physical strength. They did not know Nikki! Nor did any of them have the slightest idea that he had deliberately contracted cholera in order to put his mind over matter theory to the test. Once he had what seemed to him conclusive proof that his mind and will could dictate even to the point of difference between death and life, he emerged from the self-imposed test with all the high spirits of a victorious prizefighter after a decisive victory. So great was this sense of triumph that it erased from Nikola's mind the real purpose for which he had risked his life. It was his father who reminded him of it.

The Reverend Tesla came into his son's room early one morning about a week after that crucial day and stood at the bedside looking at Nikola solemnly.

"Good morning. Father," Nikki said cheerfully.

His father did not answer. He merely shook his head sadly and sighed.

"What's wrong. Father?" Nikki asked, sitting up in bed. "Is anyone—is Mother—?"

The Reverend Tesla placed a large hand on his son's chest and gently pushed him back onto his pillow. "I'm sorry to see you looking so pale and wan, my boy."

"But, Father, I feel fi—"

"I know you like to put up a brave front," the Reverend Tesla interrupted quickly. "I know you want to spare your mother's feelings and mine. But you don't fool me. I know you're still critically ill. But it wouldn't be right for you to try to fool Dr. Reichsbahn, who is coming this morning to examine you before signing a certificate of disability for the army."

Nikki realized at once that his father was trying to warn him of the pitfall toward which his pride had been leading him. He stared at his father in amazement, wanting to grin or laugh outright or at least say, "Thanks for the hint." But there was not a sign of a twinkle in the Reverend Tesla's eyes as he continued to gaze upon his son gravely and a little sorrowfully.

Nikki clasped his fingers across his chest and stared at the ceiling. "I guess I just don't know my own weakness," he sighed.

"Don't be surprised if Dr. Reichsbahn insists that you are so weakened by your illness that you must have complete rest fora year," the Reverend Tesla said gravely.

"A year! A whole year!" Nikki exclaimed and sat up again.

His father stared at him reprovingly, and he sank back on the pillows. "Not a whole year?" he asked pleadingly.

"A whole year," his father repeated inexorably. "A year in which people must see you taking it easy, lazing in the sun, fishing, or possibly letting me teach you the noble game of billiards. We must be certain that no question is raised about your inability to do strenuous work."

It was blackmail, Nikki thought, but a gentle kind of blackmail and intended only for his good. Besides, his father had the upper hand. Nikki sighed.

"Very well, Father," he said with a sigh. "One year."

Now, at last, his father smiled and the twinkle came into his dark brown eyes.

"It's just as well," he said. "The Polytechnic Institute could not accept you for this year anyway. The quota is filled. They have accepted you for next year. You have already been registered. Now, now! Don't sit up! Don't shout! You'll bring on a relapse!"

Once having accepted the fact that he must rest, Nikola was surprised to discover that he really needed to. The illness had taken much more out of him than he had realized, and he found that he was grateful for the opportunity to lie on a wicker couch in the sun, wrapped in an afghan his mother had knitted for him, reading novels and books it would never otherwise have occurred to him to read. The neighbors and many of the Reverend Tesla's parishioners, as soon as they discovered that their first tentative overtures were received graciously and pleasantly by the tall, somewhat formidable looking young invalid, were quick to bring him fruit and lend him books from their libraries. It was thus that he happened to read Mark Twain's A Connecticut Yankee in King Arthur's Court, which he found so stimulating, as well as amusing, that he honestly felt it was the cause of a reawakened interest in life outside a laboratory.

Even the Countess con Filibustering came to call on him! She told him that she and her husband, the Mayor, had talked things over and they both wanted him to know that they were his friends and were very proud of his scholastic record. Nikola, embarrassed and feeling guilty because of his long nurtured dislike of this woman who had been so unkind to him, did not know what to say. He could not very well apologize to her for his many unspoken thoughts. Lie surprised him further by telling them that, when he had recovered sufficiently, there would be an easy job waiting for him in the library. He could only stammer his thanks.

After she had gone, he began to reevaluate some of his ideas. Perhaps he had not been right to exclude friendship and kindliness from his life. Perhaps one could allow oneself to like people and accept their kindness. The more he thought about it, the more convinced he became that neighborliness, kindliness, even friendships, could be included in his life—as long as no emotional demands were made on him. A scientist could not afford to be distracted by problems created by a strong feeling of obligation to a friend—and he must certainly be on his guard against the bonds of love.

After coming to this conclusion, he felt better about opening the carefully wrapped gift that the Countess con Filibustering had brought him. It was a book, beautifully bound in green Morocco leather, containing colored drawings and steel engravings of many of the great wonders of the world. His father, crossing the lawn that separated the church from the back of the Teslas' house, waved at his son, but received no answering wave. He walked over, stood behind Nikola's couch, and looked over his shoulder to see what it was that held the boy's rapt attention. Nikola was staring at a picture of Niagara Falls. He became aware of his father's presence behind him and, looking around, he smiled.

"Someday I'm going to harness that waterfall," he said.

The Reverend Tesla came around the couch and smiled down at his son. "You're beginning to feel better, I see. Don't you think it's time we began the serious study of billiards?"

Billiards turned out to be the ideal game for Nikola. He found that he could visualize in advance the various angles of impact that would be needed to guide the three balls along the courses he wished them to take. His unusually long thumbs helped him to guide the cue with deadly accuracy. It was not many weeks before he could beat every opponent who dared challenge him. When this happened, he lost most of his interest in the game and played only occasionally with his father, more because he realized it gave pleasure to the Reverend Tesla than because of any fun he himself derived from it.

Soon he was able to start working in the library. The job there served three purposes very well: It provided a small amount of money with which he could pay at least part of the cost of his illness; it gave him an excuse to begin work on his memory training; and it also gave him an opportunity to obtain and take home with him the most recent works on electricity.

His mother's memory never failed to astonish him. She might not be able to remember the color of a neighbor's dress five minutes after the visitor had departed. But, on the other hand, she could repeat a whole chapter of the Connecticut Yankee after Nikola had read it to her just once—despite the fact that she did not understand English and did not know the meaning of a single word she "remembered."

Nikola and his father, on the other hand, could not remember sounds. But both could read a printed page, close the book, and recite every word they had read without a single error or omission.

Nikola developed his memory still further at this time. He trained himself to make a mental index of his reading so that he could actually remember—for an indefinite period of time—the fact that on page 231 of a certain book there was a paragraph describing in detail the working parts of a dynamo. He could file this information in his memory so accurately that, if he wished to review the material, all he had to do was to recall the book and the page, visualizing the printed paragraph so clearly that he never had to refer to the actual book.

When the time came for his departure for Gratz, Austria, a year later to begin his work as a student at Polytechnic, it was almost with regret that he gave up his job at the library. No one outside the immediate family knew anything of his plans. Because he was not yet of age, he did not need a visa to leave Serbia, but it was important that the army authorities continue to think of him as an invalid. Arrangements for his departure were made very quietly, and neighbors and acquaintances were given the impression that he was merely going to the Black Forest for a much needed vacation. There was no farewell party; his parents even thought it wiser to refrain from accompanying him to the coach station. Goodbyes were exchanged briskly and casually in the living room, and he left the house with no more ado than if he had been going to work at the library. As he walked down the front steps and along the path to the street, he wanted to resist the strong impulse to turn for a final glance at his home, knowing that not all the arguments in the world could keep his mother away from the window. Not to wave goodbye would be to hurt her as much as he had once hurt Keno. He turned and waved cheerfully.

The year of enforced rest had done Nikola a great deal of good. He was in better physical condition than he had ever been, and he plunged into the new curriculum with tremendous energy. He allowed himself only four hours' sleep each night. He developed the habit of reading and studying until eleven, when he retired; at three he arose refreshed and began tackling the more difficult problems in his homework. Classes at the institute began at eight. His heavy schedule enabled him to pass his exams in nine subjects at the end of the first term—no one else in his class was enrolled in more than five courses. Without exception, his teachers marveled at his diligence and brilliance.

The dean of the Technical Faculty wrote to the Reverend Tesla, at the end of Nikola's first term:

Your son's ability to read and converse in four languages, and to read them with complete understanding of even the most idiomatic phrases—his brilliance in the laboratory and his excellence in all forms of mathematics have impressed every member of the faculty. Your son is a star of the first magnitude.

During the summer Nikola took account of himself and the progress he was making. Looking back over the past year, he came to the conclusion that he had been behaving rather like a child let loose in a candy shop. He had stuffed himself full of gum drops, allay suckers, jelly beans, chocolate creams, caramels, and anything else that came to hand, swallowing them all in such rapid succession that each individual candy lost its flavor and simply blended into a general sweetness. He decided that it was high time to take a more mature view of his curriculum and so, in his second year, he limited himself to courses in mathematics, mechanics, and physics.

This proved to be a wise and most fortunate decision, for it gave young Tesla more time to concentrate on solving some of the more difficult and intricate problems that were presented to him that term.

Physics had always been his favorite subject and he had always been lucky in the professors assigned to him in those courses. At Polytechnic, his physics professor was Dr. Poeschl. It was he who seemed only to wave his hand in order to accomplish the minor miracles which were in every instance examples or proofs of the major miracles they served to demonstrate. It was Professor Poeschl who introduced Nikola to his nemesis—the Gramme machine.

CHAPTER 8

THE GRAMME MACHINE was a piece of electrical equipment sent to the institute from Paris. It could be used as either a dynamo or a motor. If turned by mechanical power, it generated electricity; if supplied with electricity, it operated as a motor and produced mechanical power. The machine fascinated Nikola from the first moment he saw it in operation. He liked its neat compactness and the ingenuity that had gone into its construction. He found it disappointing in only one respect.

"I should think that so much sparking would cause waste of power," he stated.

"It is unavoidable," Professor Poeschi answered. "As long as electricity flows in one direction, and as long as a magnet has two poles—each of which acts opposingly on the current—we will always have to use a commutator to change the direction of the current in the rotating armature at precisely the right moment. Thus far no one has been able to figure out how to make or use a commutator that does not give off sparks."

"I know that," Nikola answered a little impatiently. "What I meant was, why do we have to have a commutator?"

Professor Poeschi shoved his spectacles clear up to the top of his head and stared at Nikola as if inspecting a test tube containing a liquid that had just turned smoky when it should have remained clear.

"Very humorous—very humorous indeed!" he said with no attempt to veil his sarcasm.

"I wasn't trying to be funny," Nikola protested. "I just thought—"

Professor Poeschi held up his hand for silence. "Just a moment, Tesla—or perhaps I should say 'Mr. Tesla' to so profound a student—" He turned to the other members of the class. "Do any of you feel the compulsion to eliminate a commutator from the modem motor?" he asked.

Everyone shook his head. Someone laughed. Again the professor raised his hand for silence.

"No, no!" he exclaimed. "This is no laughing matter. One of our ordinarily conscientious students wishes this information. Will one of you gentlemen kindly explain the function of a commutator to our Mr. Tesla?"

Nikola started to protest, but Professor Poeschi, silencing him with a look, turned to smile benignly on a student who had stood up and was quite evidently anxious to impress the professor and the other members of the class with his own knowledge of motors and their operation. What was particularly annoying to Nikola was the fact that he had always regarded— and continued to regard—this boy as a "cabbage head."

"The first sources of electrical current were batteries," the youth began pompously. Nikola shuddered. Professor Poeschl's eyes twinkled mischievously as he saw Nikola bite his lip. The pompous one continued: "Batteries produced a small, steady flow. When man sought to produce electricity from mechanical power, he sought to make the same kind the batteries produced—a steady flow in one direction."

Again Nikola tried to interrupt and again was silenced.

"Very interesting. Very instructive," Professor Poeschi said, nodding encouragingly. "Please continue."

"The kind of current a dynamo produces when coils of wire are whirled in a magnetic field is not this kind of current. It flows first in one direction, then in the opposite direction. The commutator was invented in order to make this alternating current come out in one direct flow. Without it the motor—which depends on a flow of uninterrupted direct current—cannot operate."

"Excellent! Excellent!" beamed Professor Poeschl. He turned to Nikola. "Does that clarify the situation for you, Tesla?"

"I find the gentleman's explanation most adequate, sir" Nikola replied with surprising meekness. Professor Poeschl looked at him suspiciously. It was not like this intense young firebrand, whom he both liked and respected, to take things lying down. "Have I your permission to ask him just one question?" Nikola asked and the professor nodded.

"Why must the motor be operated on direct current? Couldn't we eliminate the commutator if we could devise a means of operating the motor on alternating current—the kind that is, as the gentleman says, now produced by all the dynamos manufactured?"

Unexpectedly Professor Poeschl threw back his head and laughed so heartily that his glasses flew off the top of his headando it was only by a miracle that he rescued them unbroken. With the glasses safely back on his nose, he addressed the class:

"You see before you an excellent example of a young man with a fixation other words, a very stubborn and obstinate young man." He continued more seriously. "Mr. Tesla will, in my opinion, one day accomplish great things. But this is certainly one thing he will never accomplish! What he proposes is, well, it's as if we could convert the steady pulling power of gravity, for instance, into a rotary push or pull. It's an impossible idea."

Nikola raised his hand.

"Now now Tesla," Professor Poeschl admonished, don't push me too far. Don't make me lose my temper. Well, out with it? What is it now?"

"Isn't it true that the 'steady pulling power of gravity, which you just mentioned, makes the moon go around the earth and the earth revolve around the sun?"

Professor Poeschl stared at Nikola for a moment. His mouth opened, no words came out. Then he turned to the class.

"I'm changing tomorrow's assignment. Instead of taking up the question of sound transmission, as I had previously announced, we will spend the entire time in a discussion of Mr. Tesla's remarkable but impossible theory."

Instead of discouraging Nikola, this ridicule had the opposite effect. His new schedule of classes allowed him more free time and he spent most of it in summoning up pictures of dynamos or motors operating smoothly and silently, fed by alternating, instead of direct, current.

He recalled his unsuccessful attempt to make a flying machine by means of a vacuum powered cylinder. He remembered what he had learned from that failure—that the angle at which the driving force struck the cylinder was the important factor in determining both the speed and continuity of the cylinder's motion. He visualized a force that could strike the cylinder successively as the cylinder revolved. But he struggled in vain. When graduation day came a year later, he had still not been able to prove his theory or make Professor Poeschi change his mind.

Immediately following the graduation ceremony, while packing his clothes and few personal belongings in his tiny fifth floor room in the big dormitory, Nikola was surprised to hear the sound of heavy footsteps on the stairway. Who could be coming up all those stairs to see him, he wondered? Since he had stuck to his resolution to give up the distracting luxury of friends and casual acquaintances in order to concentrate on his studies, he couldn't think of a single soul who would want to say goodbye. But the footsteps stopped outside his room. There was a knock. Nikola's long legs carried him to the door in two strides and he flung it open.

"You certainly manage to make yourself inaccessible, Tesla," Professor Poeschi panted. "It's been so many years since I've climbed five flights of stairs, I'd forgotten what it was like. Well, aren't you going to let me in, now that I've got here?"

"Forgive me!" Nikola exclaimed. "It's just that I'm so surprised to see you. I was thinking about you, you see, and—please come in."

Nikola almost leaped across the room to the one chair that the room boasted. Hurriedly he lifted a pile of books he had put there ready for packing, and placed them on the desk. He turned around to find his visitor grinning at him. He looked from the spindly little chair in his hands to the tremendous girth of the florid, still panting professor, and put the chair down again.

"I think it would be safer for me to sit on the bed," Professor Poeschi said. "I don't want you to have to pay a bill for damages on your last day here."

The bedsprings squeaked and squealed as if in protest, as the old man sank down. Nikola straddled the chair and sat waiting for an explanation of this unexpected visit. As soon as he had caught his breath, Professor Poeschi obliged.

"Nikola," he began, and interrupted himself. "I don't suppose you mind my calling you by your first name, now that you've graduated, do you?"

Nikola shook his head.

"Not that I intend to presume upon your courtesy in allowing me to intrude upon your privacy this way," his visitor continued. "I shall not ask if we may be friends. I know that neither of us is anxious to have friends. They waste too much valuable time, don't they, Nikola? No, I came to make a confession."

He paused. Nikola said nothing, wondering how the professor, who had seemed to pay him scant attention, could possibly have guessed his secret thoughts.

"I'm certain that ever since I gave you that verbal spanking when you were a sophomore, you've had it in for me."

Nikola started to protest, but the professor waved him into silence and continued. "Don't deny it. No matter what else you've been doing, you've thought almost constantly about the operation of an alternating current motor. And every time you've failed to come up with a solution and have been tempted to drop the whole blasted thing, a whole crew of snarling, sneering, little devils—all wearing spectacles on top of their nasty little heads—have begun poking you in the posterior with their sharp little pitchforks, and back to it you went, having another try at that elusive solution! Well, here's my confession, Nikola. I think your idea is right."

"You do!" Nikola exclaimed and stood up so suddenly that the chair fell over,

"Yes, my boy, I do. I don't know what the solution is, and I'm sure I've thought about it almost as much as you have. I know it sounds crazy, and so I don't mention my belief—your belief—to any of my colleagues. But I believe in the possibility of eliminating the need for a commutator by the use of alternating current. What's more, I believe you're going to discover it if you keep on trying long enough and hard enough. And that brings me to the favor I want to ask of you."

"A favor? Of course, if there's anything—"

"I want you to promise me you'll let me know at once when you do find the answer."

"I promise," Nikola said without hesitating an instant.

"There's one more thing, Nikola," he said. "In the event that you do find the answer, I'd like to feel that you're not too far away so that you could get in touch with me quickly. I know you're planning to go to Prague University in the fall, but how would you feel about a job in the meantime? A friend of mine owns a big tool and die factory at Maribor—less than ten miles from here. He needs a man who's good at math and has more than a working knowledge of mechanics to supervise the making of some new electrical equipment. He would be willing to pay sixty florins a month."

"Sixty florins!"

Nikola could hardly believe his ears. He thought the professor must have said "six," not "sixty." Sixty florins! Why, that was about six times as much as the Reverend Tesla received from the church. It was a small fortune. It would enable him to pay his own tuition at the University without help from his father.

"I take it that you're not averse to giving the matter some consideration," Professor Poeschi said drily.

"It would be wonderful," Nikola replied. "When do I start?"

"Any time within the next few days, Nikola. I'll go home and write you a note that you can present to Mr. Droushka, my friend, when you go there."

"I can't thank you enough—"

"Don't try. Just remember your promise, Nikola. I want to be the first to know if you should happen to hit upon the answer." He walked over to the door and turned.

"Anyway," he said, smiling, "if you do, you'll be rid of those nasty little devils that are poking at you all the time."

Nikola's thin, narrow lips spread into one of his rare smiles. "Oh, no, I won't. They'll be there just the same. But now they'll be smiling instead of snarling and sneering."

Professor Poeschi laughed. "I wonder if your posterior will be able to tell the difference!" he said. His deep, rumbling laughter continued to fill the hall with echoes long after the top of his head had disappeared down the curving stairwell.

CHAPTER 9

THAT AUTUMN when Nikola went home for a brief visit before entering the university at Prague, his parents noticed a great difference in him. For the first time he seemed at ease and self-assured He had money in his pocket and in the bank— money he had earned himself. The excellence of his record at Polytechnic had made it possible for him to enter the university without having to take entrance exams. He had earned enough to pay not only for his tuition but also for his living expenses for the year ahead of him, and he had been assured emphatically that the job at Maribor would be held open for him the following summer.

For the first time since that day, so long ago, when he had overheard Mrs. Wentzlas talking about his brother, Nikola was not driving himself. This was quite deliberate on his part. He had failed to find the elusive answer to the problem that so perplexed him and Professor Poeschi, and he attributed his failure to over eagerness He could visualize the motor of his imagination, operating to perfection, but he could not visualize the manner in which the magnetic field could turn the armature without the sparking and sputtering caused by the current's change in direction. He decided that, if he were to relegate the whole problem to his subconscious, he might someday—when least expecting it—awaken to the entire visualization of the solution. Professor Poeschi had been disappointed but completely understanding.

"Perhaps if I stop sticking pitchforks into myself—in addition to the ones you wield—" Nikola had said to the professor when he called to say goodbye, "maybe the answer will come by itself."

"It's worth trying, Nikola. Anything's worth a try. I know you'll hit upon it someday. I only hope—" He stopped speaking suddenly.

"What is it?" Nikola asked. "What were you going to say?"

"No. I won't say it. It was just another kind of pitchfork. I won't inflict it on you, Nikola."

And he flatly refused to say any more.

The courses he had selected at the university—English literature, advanced mathematics, and electrical engineering—were sufficiently difficult to hold his attention, yet not so demanding that he felt himself under pressure. That "nature abhors a vacuum" had been one of the very first things he had learned in the physics class at the Real Gymnasium. He believed that, if he succeeded in maintaining a vacuum in his heart, ideas— such as the solution of the alternating current problem—might rush in to fill it. In the meantime, with the self-discipline he had carefully developed, he found it a simple matter to limit his interests and enthusiasms to those studies and occupations and acquaintances that were likely to make few demands upon his emotions. He renewed his billiard playing and, for a time, again found the game exciting and challenging. But, as before, when he had succeeded in beating all challengers, from both the student body and the faculty, he lost interest. It was then that he became acquainted with chess.

Here was a game that presented constantly changing sets of problems, depending on the opponent's technique and skill. Nikola found that, with his sense of visualization, he could often foresee his adversary's moves far enough in advance to work out a counterattack, and it was not long before he had acquired considerable fame as an expert. He organized a university chess team, which challenged teams from other colleges and schools, and so actually instituted intercollegiate activities, which up to that time were completely unheard of.

Late in the spring of his final year of the three year course, Nikola received a letter from his father telling him that he and Mrs. Tesla planned to come to Prague for their son's graduation exercises. Mrs. Tesla, he wrote, had always wanted to see Prague, and they both wanted to have the pleasure of seeing their son receive the high honors that he had written them about.

Nikola was delighted and spent the following weeks doing small errands to assure his parents' comfort and entertainment both at the university and in the city.

Then, just a week before the day of their expected arrival, he received a letter from his father saying that they would be unable to come. The Reverend Tesla explained in great detail how the minister whom he had engaged to substitute for him at the services that Sunday had fallen ill. Also, the bishop had been prevailed upon to speak at the Real Gymnasium graduation exercises and might be offended if the Reverend Tesla was not in town to greet him. Plausible reasons they seemed, and Nikola took them at face value. He understood, too, that his mother would not want to come alone. She would not want to see the wonders of Prague for the first time without being able to share the thrills and pleasures with her husband.

On the day of the commencement Nikola sat on the platform with some sixty other members of the graduating class. He was paying scant attention to the glowing words of hope that were being uttered, with impassioned gestures, by the valedictorian. The words were not new to him, nor were the thoughts and ideas being so ardently presented. He had spent many hours helping the young man write the speech.

His attention wandered and he glanced down at the empty seats in the third row: the two he had reserved for his parents. He felt a moment's guilt for having forgotten to tell the authorities that he would not need them and that someone else might use them. As he gazed idly at the vacant seats, his mind began to play him tricks. He saw his mother and father sitting in the audience! They were listening to the speaker with rapt attention. It seemed to Nikola that his father's eyes wavered from the speaker to glance at him. The Reverend Tesla smiled and nodded almost imperceptibly. His mother's attention never faltered; she was watching the speaker's every gesture as if her life depended on not losing a precious syllable. Enthusiastic hand clapping aroused Nikola to awareness that the speech was finished. The speaker, bowed, acknowledging the applause, and bowed again. Then he came over and sat down next to Nikola.

"We did it, Tesla! We did it! It went like a house afire, didn't it?"

"They certainly seemed to like it," Nikola agreed absentmindedly.

"Whew! I don't mind telling you I'm glad that's over and done with." His classmate sighed, wiping his perspiring face with a large handkerchief.

Nikola nodded and glanced once more at the seats in the third row. His father was still applauding, but his mother had risen. She was the only person in the whole auditorium who had not remained seated to await the awarding of diplomas. She was not only on her feet—she was pushing her way past the others in the row, trying to reach the aisle. All the while she moved sideways, crowding past the knees of the other proud parents, she kept her face turned toward the platform, an urgent plea in her deepest eyes. Her lips were drawn together tightly as if she were trying to repress tears, and she was beckoning to him, urging him to come down off the platform and go with her.

Suddenly he was conscious of a loud shuffling of feet, and someone poked his shoulder. The whole class was on its feet, moving in single file toward the lectern where the president was handing out diplomas in alphabetical order. Nikola was near the end of the line, but his six-feet-two inches enabled him to peer over the heads of the others in front of him. Both seats were empty.

He could not put out of his mind the look of urgent appeal he had seen on his mother's face. A feeling within him grew that something was wrong at home. Possibly she was seriously ill and hoping desperately that her son would come home before it was too late. Nikola felt that he must leave at once—catch the first train. Since no railroad ran to Go spic, he would have to change to a coach at the nearest junction. He had not intended to leave Prague for two days. There was the senior dance on the following night, as well as a series of small parties that would go on for several more days. To some of these he had accepted invitations, but everything seemed unimportant to him now as he waited what seemed an endless time until his name was called.

"Nikola Tesla."

At last! He hurried forward, almost running in his eagerness to have the ceremony over with. It was evident that the president had intended to single Nikola out for special commendation, for he held a slip of paper with notes of what he planned to say. Extending the diploma with his right hand, the president glanced at the notes in his left.

"It gives us the greatest possible pleasure—" he began but got no further. Nikola took the diploma from the outstretched hand, said, "Thank you very much," and walked quickly off the platform and out of the auditorium.

On the way to his room, he suddenly remembered that he had not drawn much money from his bank account for the week end, and therefore would have to borrow money for his fare home. Then, realizing that he could write a check, he changed course and headed rapidly for the treasurer's office, where he knew they would accommodate him. But it was closed. Fretting and fuming at the delay, he went from one small store to another, cashing small amounts until he had accumulated enough for the fare.

He wasted no more time but threw his belongings into two suitcases, stacking some things in a corner with the idea of having them shipped to him at a later date, and hurried to the station.

Less than three hours after he had removed his diploma from the president's limp grasp, Nikola was on a train, looking back for the last time at the old, ivy covered buildings and the tree shaded campus. He arrived at Go spic at dusk on the following afternoon.

The little coach station seemed to him much smaller than he had remembered. There was no hansom cab in sight and, feeling an urgency he could not explain, he started to walk. The station was a little more than a mile from the Tesla home.

Nikola set out with great strides, swinging his two heavy suit cases backward and forward rhythmically so that their weight and impetus seemed to propel him forward.

"Nikola! Nikola Tesla!"

It was a woman's voice and it came from behind him. Not wanting to take the time to stop and exchange greetings, he pretended not to hear, but continued on his way without a break in the rhythm of the swinging suitcases. When the voice called out again, this time accompanied by the sound of horses' hoofs on crunching gravel, he realized that it came from a carriage. It was the Countess con Furstenburg in a smart black and white phaeton driven by a liveried coachman. As the impressive rig pulled alongside Nikola, the lady leaned out and called again:

"Nikolai Won't you let me give you a lift? I'm going right past your house."

It would save precious time, he thought; besides, his arms and shoulders were beginning to ache from carrying the heavy bags. He had not realized how heavy they actually were until he saw the strapping coachman tumble with them as he tried to hoist them onto the high front seat. Nikola sank onto the tufted seat beside the Countess and, leaning back, closed his eyes for just a moment.

"You poor boy, you must be exhausted," she exclaimed. "I'm sure you didn't sleep a wink all night. I know I never can on those sooty trains and dusty stages."

He opened his eyes to look at her. "Thank you for the lift," he said courteously, "It will get me home much faster."

"Of course it will," she answered, "and every minute counts. Oh Nikola, we're all so sorry for you. It's wonderful that you could get here so quickly. Your mother's been asking for you —hoping and praying that you'd get here before—"

Nikola stared at her. It was his mother then! Something had happened. An accident? A sudden illness? He would not ask because he couldn't admit that he had not known, and had rushed home only because of a premonition. His father would not want him to tell her anything that would seem so irreligious. He said nothing but just sat staring at the fat red neck of the coachman in front of him.

The carriage was slowing down. They must be almost there. Yes, there was the Wentzlas house. Home was just around the corner. He stepped out of the carriage before the wheels stopped turning.

"Thank you . . . thanks very much," he said over his shoulder as he opened the white picket gate between the tall hedges. Forgetting all about his suitcases, he closed the gate softly behind him and turned. His mother was standing on the porch, with that same tight, drawn look he had seen on her face at the commencement exercises. She was slowly pounding her fist into the open palm of her other hand, rhythmically, intently, as if she were urging on a runner in a race. So great was her concentration that she neither heard nor saw her son as he hurried up the path.

"Mother," he called softly in a tone one would use to a sleepwalker.

She looked down and saw him. The tautness left her face, to be replaced by a stare of sheer disbelief and wonder. Then, suddenly and without warning, she fell against the post that supported the porch roof, slid down its full length to the floor. In one great leap Nikola was beside her, holding her around the waist. Her eyes opened, but for a moment they were unseeing.

"I must have fainted," she said wonderingly. "That's the first time in my life it ever happened. It's strange—like—"Suddenly realization came as she remembered why she had fainted.

"Nikki, oh Nikki!" she exclaimed. "You did hear me, didn't you? You've come. Oh thank God, you've come!"

"Is it—Father?" Nikola asked fearfully.

She nodded.

"Is he—"

"Yesterday afternoon the doctor told me that it was just a matter of a few hours, at most. It was then I prayed that you might come. He's been asking for you. He has so much he wants to say to you. Oh Nikki—"

For a moment she clutched him convulsively and held him close. She seemed to draw strength from him, for after a moment she stepped back. "I feel ashamed of myself, Nikki. I didn't think my prayer was heard—I didn't believe it would bring you here in time. So I played the game we used to play. Remember, when you were little? I would stay in one room and you in another and I'd think hard about something. Then you would try to guess what I was thinking? Don't tell Father about this, will you, Nikki? I wouldn't want him to know I doubted that my prayer would be heard."

He shook his head. Together they crossed the porch and went into the hallway. Neither of them heard the coachman as he set down the bags.

"No, not upstairs, Nikki," his mother said. "Father's in his study. We fixed up a bed tor him there to spare him the climb."

The Reverend Tesla opened his eyes and smiled as Nikola opened the door of the study.

"I thought I heard your voice, Nikki, but I was afraid I was just hearing things. Come here, boy. Sit on the bed. Let me look at you. Oh, I've so much I want to say—"

Nikola sat on the bed.

"You know I'm dying?"

Nikola nodded. It did not occur to him to offer polite reassurances. There had never been any pretense between him and his father.

"I wish you believed, as I do, that we will meet again, in another, a better, world."

"I don't—I just can't, Father."

"Scientist," his father chided him gently. "I'm afraid that you will find life lonely and empty unless you learn to believe. I can be content because I know we shall all be together again."

"You will be with me always. Father. When I miss you or need your advice, I have but to think of you to summon you. And there you are, so real that I can sense your nearness."

"I'll be waiting for your call, Nikki. Take care of your mother. I've arranged to have Mother go to live with Mrs. Wentzlas. She will be less lonely . . . There will be enough so that she need not want, but if you make a great deal of money —well, I should like her to have the luxuries I couldn't give her."

Nikki nodded.

"There's something more. I've wanted to say it for a long time, but I lacked the courage. It's easier to be frank when you're dying, Nikki. I've wanted to tell you that I admire your honesty and integrity. If you keep those, you will always behave according to God's teachings, no matter what you believe. There!" He smiled and sighed. "That's said. Now, I'm sleepy, Nikki. Ease the pillow a bit, will you, boy?"

Nikola adjusted the pillow.

"Ask your mother to come in, Nikki."

Then, as Nikola started to tiptoe from the sickroom, the Reverend Tesla called to him and he came back to the bedside.

"I forgot one last thing, Nikki. I've meant to tell you— about your brother Dane. Your mother and I always feared we'd be punished through you because of our attitude toward him."

"I don't understand. Father."

"We took pride in Dane. He reflected his glory upon us and we boasted, but we both knew that it was our vanity. We didn't understand him, as we do you. We feared you would be taken from us because we had proven ourselves unworthy. . .

CHAPTER 10

NIKOLA HAD INTENDED taking two more years of specialized training, but his father's death made it necessary for him to begin earning money at once. The job at Maribor had been completed. With the growing interest throughout Europe in electricity and its as-yet little understood uses, Nikola expected little difficulty in obtaining a job. Armed with his diploma from the university and letters of enthusiastic recommendation from his former employer in Maribor, as well as from Professor Poeschi and the president of the university, he traveled to Budapest where there were several distant relatives and friends of his father.

Like many graduates before him—and millions who would follow, he was due for a rude and harsh awakening: there were no jobs available. The seething, thriving city of Budapest had managed to get along very well without young Nikola Tesla, and the feeling seemed to be widespread that it could continue to do so.

Everywhere he went he heard much talk of the new invention of an American scientist named Bell. Alexander Graham Bell's telephone would revolutionize Europe, people said. It would soon be possible to talk to people hundreds of miles away through use of this new means of transmitting sound. Nikola wanted very much to become associated with the development of this invention, but found that it was still only in the discussion stage. He learned, however, that when, at some future unnamed date, something would be done about it. Such action could be under the supervision of the Hungarian government's Central Telegraph Office. He applied for a job there and was offered the opportunity to become one of several draftsmen at a salary so small that he could barely live on it. He accepted it because of his interest in the telephone.

This proved to be a wise decision, for it was not long before his outstanding ability attracted the attention of his superiors. He was transferred to another department and found himself working on calculations and estimates of the cost of telephone installations. Again his diligence and ability stood him in good stead. In 1881, when the first telephone exchange was established in Budapest, he was placed in charge of it. He was given a week's vacation and traveled at once to Smiljan to tell his mother that on his twenty fifth birthday he had been made the manager—in full charge—of an important engineering enterprise.

In connection with his work at the telephone exchange, Nikola had to listen to and subsequently analyze complaints. Reports of any inadequacy or failure of the instruments installed came to his desk. It was in this way that he became aware of the many protests from customers who claimed to have great difficulty in hearing the speakers at the other end. Voices were faint and there seemed to be a great deal of crackling and other noises exploding in their ears much of the time. Upon investigation of these complaints, Nikola discovered that they were often justified. He set to work on an invention that would both magnify the sound of the voice and reduce the irrelevant sounds which he felt were due to "static" electricity. The finished device, his first invention, was called the "telephone repeater" or amplifier, but which today would be more accurately described as a loudspeaker. It was unquestionably the forerunner of the sound producer now in use in every home radio set. Nikola was very proud of it. He had every right to be, for even many years later the ingenuity and design of his 1881 invention compared favorably with those developed more than thirty years later. This invention was never patented but it was put into immediate use by the Budapest Telephone Company.

During the year he worked on the amplifier, he had as an assistant a young man named Szigeti, who, Nikola discovered, spent much of his free time reading poetry. Nikola at first looked down his long nose upon what seemed to him to be a foolish and rather effeminate pastime. He offered to teach the young man how to play billiards as a substitute for his off time interest. Szigeti learned to play billiards quite passably during the weeks that followed, but, while he was learning, he managed to arouse Nikola's interest in poetry to such an extent that he began to attempt to write it. The mathematical exactness demanded by the sonnet form appeared to him to be a charming challenge, and he worked at it with all the energy and enthusiasm that he always put into everything he tackled.

Nikola found the company of Szigeti pleasant without being in any way demanding. There would never be any danger of Szigeti wanting to develop their relationship into a lifelong friendship. He was Tesla's assistant and thought of himself as such. He knew a lot about poetry, but he also was, first and foremost, an intelligent assistant, a capable engineer. Nikola came to look forward to the occasional billiard games, the dis- cessions of Goethe and Shakespeare, and, once in a great while, walks in the country.

In February, about a year after his invention of the amplifier, Nikola, suffering from a brief illness, stayed home from the office. After work Szigeti stopped by to see if there were any thing his boss wanted. When Nikola said he felt like getting some fresh air, Szigeti suggested a walk in the park. The two young men started out at a leisurely pace toward the famous, hilly Budapest Park. On one of the higher hills they paused to admire the sunset. A poem of Goethe's about the sunset came to mind and Nikola began to recite it from memory. Abruptly he broke off and Szigeti, turning to him to see the reason for the sudden silence, was surprised and frightened by the look on his companion's face. Nikola stood transfixed, staring straight into the sun.

"What is it, Tesla? What's wrong?"

Nikola did not answer, and Szigeti grasped his arm and shook him as one might try to awaken a person in a trance. "Mr. Tesla, don't you hear me?" he cried, his voice rising as his anxiety grew.

Nikola's shook off Szigeti's arm. "Watch me," he said softly. "Don't speak. Just watch me. See, I can reverse it!"

"Mr. Tesla, are you ill? I don't see anything. Do you think you can reverse the sun?"

"Don't you see it? Look, it's right here in front of me. See how smoothly it's running! Now I throw this switch—and I reverse it. It goes just as smoothly in the opposite direction. No sparking, no loss!"

"Perhaps we'd better sit down and rest for a little while, Mr. Tesla. You've been ill—"

Nikola turned to his assistant and seemed to be seeing him for the first time.

"It's all right, Szigeti. Don't look at me as if I were the village idiot! I'm talking about my alternating current motor. I've solved the problem! The answer was there all the time. It's so simple. Just stop talking. Listen and watch. It's right here before us. It's the rotating magnetic field that is the answer! How could I have been so blind so long! Look, the rotating magnetic field drags the armature around with it! That's all! Isn't that ridiculous? All these years—and there it was all the time! So simple! So sublimely simple!"

Suddenly Szigeti realized what Nikola was saying. The beauty and simplicity of the idea hit him with almost as much force as it had hit Nikola himself.

"I think it's I who needs to sit down," he said.

Nikola followed him to a bench and picked up a twig that lay nearby.

"Szigeti, long ago I taught myself to visualize objects and formulas so that I can work on them even when they are not actually before me. In some sense, they are actually before me. But I shouldn't expect you to be able to see it too. I'll draw it for you here on the ground and I'll give you an example."

"I know what you mean by the rotating field, Mr. Tesla. I know that it will work. I don't quite see how, but—"

"I'll show you," Nikola exclaimed. "Look" And he began to draw a diagram in the dirt in front of the bench. "In all my thinking I have always used only one circuit. That has been my trouble. It is like a steam engine with one cylinder. Look."

He drew a diagram of a cylinder attached to a shaft. "You see the piston stalls for an instant on dead center both at the top and bottom of the stroke."

"I see! Go on!"

Nikola's excitement was infectious and Szigeti leaned forward to watch the grooves and circles made by the moving twig.

"I add a second cylinder. The pistons in the two cylinders are connected to the shaft so that their cranks are at an angle to each other. Now do you see what happens? The two pistons reach the top and bottom of the stroke at different times. When one is on dead center, the other is turning the engine with a power thrust."

Szigeti nodded. "That is obvious. But I don't see—"

"Using a second circuit is like adding the second cylinder to the steam engine," Nikola explained impatiently. "Don't you see? The two circuits will carry the same frequency alternating current, but the current waves will be out of step with each other—like the pistons. You must see. It is so simple!"

"I do. I do see!" Szigeti exclaimed and Nikola dropped the twig and leaned his head against the back of the bench. He closed his eyes and spoke in a calmer tone.

"The trouble has always been the single circuit. The magnetic field produced by alternating current has changed as rapidly as the current. So, instead of producing a one-direction turning force, the magnetic field just churned up a lot of useless movement—first in one direction, then in the other. That is what caused both sparking and vibration."

"I see! Of course!" Szigeti repeated, but Nikola, his eyes still closed, his long legs stretched out before him, seemed to have forgotten the other man's existence. Szigeti lapsed into silence. Presently Nikola began speaking, but more to himself than to the young man beside him.

"I will produce a field of force that rotates at high speed. It will surround and embrace an armature which will require no electrical connections' The rotating field will transfer its power, without wires, through space, feeding energy by means of its lines of force to closed circuit coils on an armature, enabling it to build up its own magnetic field that locks it into the rotating magnetic whirlwind produced by the field coils. No wires! No faulty connections! No commutator! Commutator!"

He leaped to his feet as the startled Szigeti looked at him in renewed alarm.

"I must go back to the exchange!" Nikola announced.

"The exchange! But why? There is no lab there. You can't possibly—"

"I must go there to keep a promise!"

He explained no further but started walking with long strides in the direction of the office. Szigeti jogged along at his side, hard put to keep pace with him, for Nikola seemed to be walking on air.

"Now I can die happy," Nikola exclaimed as the two reached the busy roadway. "But I mustn't allow myself that pleasure. I must live. I must return to work—my own work! I must build the alternating current motor so that I can give it to the world. It will set the world free! No longer will men have to strain and push and pull and sweat as slaves to the hard labor that has to be done. My motor will do it for them. My motor will set them free!"

When they arrived at the Telephone Exchange Building, Nikola turned to his somewhat breathless companion. "I want to thank you, Szigeti. You have been patient and kind. There is no need for you to wait for me, I may be some little time."

"But you have been ill. You are still weak. Don't you think you might need me just in case—"

"Ill? Weak? I'm as strong as an ox—as powerful as Atlas. Don't wait for me. Stop around later, if you wish, and we can talk."

Szigeti shook his head somewhat dubiously, but he left and Nikola entered the building. He stopped beside one of the operators.

"I'm going to my office," he said. "Please put through a call for me and connect it to the extension in my office."

"Certainly, Mr. Tesla," the young man replied. "Where is the call going to?"

"To the Polytechnic Institute at Gratz. I know they have installed our instruments there because I happened to see the signed contract when the order came in."

"The call is a business call, Mr. Tesla?"

"No. Personal. See that it is deducted from my salary."

"Mr. Tesla, you're the manager. You know employees are not allowed to make personal calls outside the city from this ex change."

"Suppose you take that up with the manager tomorrow, Bernhard. In the meantime, please place the call."

He entered his office, turned on the electric light, and sat down to wait. A few minutes later the phone on his desk sounded off like a gong in a firehouse.

"Polytechnic. Administration Office here," said a voice very loudly in his ear. He wondered why people felt that they had to shout whenever they talked to someone in a distant city.

"Will you please call Professor Poeschi to the telephone?"

"I'm sorry, sir, but that won't be possible."

Nikola felt a sudden shock of fear. It had been at least four years since he had heard from his old friend. Had he died in the interim?

"Why can't you?" he asked, dreading the reply.

"Because the institute has only one trunk line. There is no extension in Professor Poeschl's house. We'd have to send a messenger."

Nikola laughed in relief. "Send a messenger, by all means!"

"You'll hold on?" the voice exclaimed. "All that time? It will cost a fortune."

"It doesn't matter. Nothing matters. Nothing matters one little bit. Just get him to the phone!"

"Very well. Hold on, please." She sounded as if she thoroughly disapproved of the whole business.

Probably thinks I'm drunk, Nikola thought cheerfully.

After a long, long wait Nikola could hear voices and then the professor's well remembered voice said, "Poeschi here. What is it?"

"This is Tesla."

"Who?"

"Tesla. Nikola Tesla. The boy you prodded with pitchforks!"

"It's nonsense. It's a lie! I never prodded you or any boy with a—oh. TESLA! My boy, have you done it? Is that why you're calling? Oh Tesla, I was afraid you'd never— I thought you'd given up. And I thought, even if you solved our old problem, you'd surely forget your promise. All this time I've kept looking in the newspapers, hoping to see an announcement. Oh Tesla, my boy, but this is wonderful! Tell me, how did you find the answer? ... A vacuum? I don't understand. What has a vacuum got to do with alternating current? Never mind. It's not important how you found the solution. The important thing is that you found it. What is it?"

"A rotating magnetic field is the key. That and using more than one current at different frequencies so that the current is Staggered and so gives out a steady one directional force."

"A rotating magnetic field! How beautiful! How simple! It locks the armature tightly within its own field, doesn't it?"

"Yes."

"Have you made a model?"

"Only in my mind, but it is made accurately and operates in silence, with an almost incredible smoothness."

"Not enough, my boy. You'll have to make a model before anyone will believe you. If I didn't know you and your amazing ability to visualize things, I wouldn't believe you either."

"I'll make models in all sizes and shapes with single current and with multiple current. It will be accepted. It must be accepted."

"What did you say about how you discovered it? Tell me, perhaps it would work for me—help me in my work here."

"After years of trying in vain to force my mind to a solution, I decided to create a vacuum in my mind, in the hope the answer would be drawn into it."

Nikola could hear the old professor laughing at the other end of the wire. "How did you go about inducing a vacuum?" he asked, still chuckling.

"The ingredients were billiards and poetry and some well-chosen, pleasant, but overstimulating acquaintances."

"I have plenty of overstimulating acquaintances," Professor Poeschi answered. "And although I'm a little old for it. I might manage to take up billiards. But poetry! No, my friend, the curriculum you outline is too obnoxious to contemplate. I shall just have to be satisfied with being a teacher who prods his students with pitchforks."

Nikola hung up the receiver and went into the main office. The operator who had put through the call was still at his board. He was figuring on a piece of paper, and seemed to be having difficulty, for he wrote, erased, wet the pencil in his mouth, and wrote again. Nikola crossed the large room to him.

"Perhaps I can help you," he said. "I was the one who worked out the rates in the first place. I know exactly what the cost is per mile per minute, and I can tell you that my call cost forty two florins and eleven pfennig."

The operator looked up at him in amazement.

"That's exactly what I got, Mr. Tesla, but I just couldn't believe it. Why, that's my salary for four weeks!"

"It's equivalent to two of mine," Nikola answered, "but it doesn't seem too important just now. I'm entitled to a two week vacation. The company can just charge it off against that. I shall be leaving. I've got another job."

"Oh. A better one, I hope?"

"Oh yes, much better. My new job is to set the world free. Good night to you."

And Nikola left the building. He was whistling, but no one —not even he—could have recognized the tune.

CHAPTER 11

THE MONTHS immediately following his great discovery were the happiest, and at the same time the most frustrating, he had ever known. He was ecstatically happy in devoting full time to the development and perfection of not only every part but also every variation of his alternating power system. It was by far his most productive period. In his mind he built dynamos, motors, transformers—every unit that might someday be needed to demonstrate the many advantages of alternating current over direct as a source of electrical power. Each separate part was measured with such accuracy that there was not a thousandth inch variation in the measurements of duplicates. These constructs—the term used by engineers to describe a working model—operated flawlessly, although they had been made without the benefit of work drawings or blueprints. But Nikola had no hope of obtaining the financial backing necessary for marketing his system. He could not show them. They existed only in his mind. The making of such constructs out of copper and iron would have cost a great deal of money and Nikola had only the fast dwindling remains of his small savings.

Having discovered that he could interest no one in Budapest in his power system, and knowing that he would soon need a job if he were to continue sending even small sums home to his mother, he was delighted when Szigeti told him of a firm in Paris that might be interested in his invention and, in any event, could certainly use his services as an electrical engineer. Nikola thought that his chances of being able to arouse interest in his invention would be far better in Paris. He packed his few belongings, wrapped his sparse notes in brown paper, and set out for France, armed with a letter from Szigeti and hopes as high as they had been when he first ventured to Budapest.

Paris! The very name held a sort of magic for Nikola. He was actually going to the city that was noted for its kindly interest in young talent—the city where, supposedly, it was never difficult to find a patron for a promising young painter or writer or, he hoped, engineer. He was not surprised that he was able to find, on the day of his arrival, an apartment on the Boulevard Saint Michel that suited his taste, his needs, and his purse. Nor was he surprised when his letter of introduction got him a job with the Continental Edison Company as "junior engineer." These things happened in Paris!

In his free time he began frequenting sidewalk cafes and the stylish hotels of the period, not because he craved drink or enjoyed the fine old wines—not because he was lonesome and sought the gaiety and companionship of young people his own age. With his characteristic simplicity and directness he went to these places for the sole purpose of finding a patron or backer for his alternating current power system. Most inventors knew the wisdom of refraining from discussing the details of their inventions until the patents had been applied for. Without working models Nikola could not even register his power system, and yet he talked about it in the greatest possible detail to anyone who looked as if he might have money enough to help in the financing. Actually, he didn't care if someone stole his idea. He knew there was a fortune to be made from it, but he had no particular interest in making money. He only wanted the world to have the benefit of his invention. He could always earn money by working.

No one stole the idea. No one thought well enough of it. He could not give it away! He knew he was walking around with one of the greatest discoveries of all time in his head and no one wanted it.

The Continental Edison Company was a French company that made and installed motors and dynamos and lighting systems under the Thomas A. Edison patents. These were all, of course, direct current equipment, and no one there was in the least interested in a new system that would require new dies, new tools, and new, differently trained men. But it they were not interested in his invention, they were very much interested in the inventor. They had learned of Nikola's great ability both as an electrical expert and as an engineer, and he soon found himself being assigned to the jobs that presented the greatest difficulties.

In the course of his "troubleshooting," Nikola became aware of certain flaws in the dynamos manufactured by his company, and almost automatically worked out the way in which these faults could be corrected. He submitted his ideas to his superiors and was granted permission to test them on some of the dynamos then under construction. Every one of his suggested changes tested out satisfactorily, and all of them were adopted by the company and incorporated in all future models. Nikola received a friendly pat on the shoulder and the assurance that the Continental Edison Company would not forget. In fact, to show their appreciation, he was given a most important task. If he could complete it successfully, there would be a handsome bonus awaiting him.

Strasbourg presented a problem unlike any he had been asked to face before. The Continental Edison Company had installed a lighting system and powerhouse at the railroad station. There had been a short circuit in the wiring and a wall of the station had been blown out. Unfortunately for all concerned, this happened at the very moment when Kaiser Wilhelm was stepping from a train that had brought him there for the dedication of the new station.

The technical part of his new job presented no problem to Nikola, but winning the confidence and cooperation of the embarrassed and angry officials was something that he knew would require the tact and charm of a diplomat or a statesman. Realizing that he would probably have to remain in Strasbourg for a much longer time than the job itself warranted, he decided to make the best of it, settle down, and do some work on his own power system. He found a machine shop near the station, sent to Paris for some materials he needed, and went to work in his spare time. When his job was finished for the day, he would hurry to his shop to continue building the actual, physical models of the machines he had so often seen in his mind's eye. It took him the better part of a year to build and assemble a motor and dynamo that would, when completed, operate on alternating instead of direct current. When, at last, the constructs were completed, he pulled the switch on his power generator—exactly as he had imagined himself doing that day more than two years ago in Budapest. And, exactly as he had "seen" it happen on that occasion, when he closed the connection, there was an instant response. The armature turned, built up to full speed in an instant, and continued to operate in complete silence. He pulled the reversing switch. The armature stopped turning for a moment and then whirled into full speed in the opposite direction. There was no vibration. There were no sparks.

The test completely confirmed the theory of the rotating magnetic field and the effectiveness of alternating current, but to Nikola, who had not one moment's doubt of the outcome of the test, this was less thrilling than the fact that he had successfully built a whole, tremendously complicated system of constructs without a single blueprint or even a freehand sketch!

The mayor of Strasbourg had taken a great liking to Nikola, and now offered to bring several wealthy and influential Strasbourgers down to Tesla's machine shop. The young engineer was delighted. Both he and Mayor Bauzin felt certain that enough interest would be aroused to warrant the formation of a stock company, which would manufacture and market the Tesla poly phase induction motor. But Nikola was doomed to disappointment. The viewers could not deny that the motor and dynamo would operate. They were actually operating. But none of them could see any great advantages in the alternating current idea.

Mayor Bauzin assured Nikola that he would find more progressive minded men in Paris, now that the constructs were available. He said that he would be willing to supervise demonstrations of the system, it Nikola chose to send anyone to Strasbourg to view the models in operation.

Nikola had every reason to look forward to his return to Paris. He now had a better chance to raise the money needed to promote the alternating current motor. Also, and more immediate, was the substantial bonus he would get for the work accomplished in Strasbourg and for the improvements he had effected in the Edison equipment. This represented an immediate opportunity to build and demonstrate more and larger models of the poly phase system.

For almost two full weeks after his return to Paris, the Continental Edison Company avoided the issue of his bonus. The president was away; the vice president didn't have the requisite authority. The treasurer had received no instructions. It all seemed quite plausible at first.

The improvements that Nikola had made for the Continental Edison equipment had saved the company thousands of dollars and would earn a great many more. The public relations job he had done in Strasbourg meant more thousands to the company. In addition to these obligations, he was offering the company first refusal on his alternating current system. Had any one of the executives had any imagination or even common sense, they would have made Nikola some sort of an offer. He would have been satisfied with very little, provided his invention was given to the world. When Nikola realized that no one had any intention of giving him anything, he became so angry that he walked into the office and gave notice, effective immediately.

One of the minor executives of the company sought him out in his quarters that evening.

"I don't blame you for being angry, Tesla," Mr. Batchellor said sympathetically. "I would be, too, if I were in your boots. But if I were you, I wouldn't stick around Paris moping about it. I'd go to America, that's what I'd do."

America! Why not? Why had he not thought of it before? America was a new country, a young country. It was quite likely that more people there would be interested in new ideas, new inventions, than were to be found in Budapest or Strasbourg or Paris.

"Tell me about it, please. Everything. The way they think— the way the people act about new things—about the chances of getting a job. I don't believe those stories of gold lying about in the streets. And even if they were true, I would still want to work," he told Mr. Batchellor.

"Well, I think a letter from me might get you a job with the Edison Company in New York, Tesla. I can't guarantee it, of course, but I can promise you it'll at least get you an interview with Thomas A. himself. After that it'd be up to you, but I think the Old Man is shrewd enough to know when it's wise to put a good man on the payroll."

"Is the Edison Company in New York in any way like the Continental Edison Company of Paris?" Nikola asked, frowning.

"As a matter of fact, it isn't," Mr. Batchellor assured him. "You see, we over here merely handle and manufacture machines built on the Old Man's patents. We lease the right to do that. But the one company has nothing to do with the other. Mr. Edison has a very small staff. He does all the hiring himself. Every college graduate, every would be engineer, every mechanic, wants to work for Edison because he's got just about the biggest thing going and because he's the biggest inventor in America."

"He will soon be the second biggest," Nikola said, smiling. "When will you be so kind as to give me that letter of introduction?"

There was a boat leaving for America a week later, Nikola learned.

"And the one after that?" Nikola asked.

The clerk in the steamship office pulled a heavy ledger out of the drawer of the desk in front of him. "Hmm," he said as he glanced down the long columns of names and reservations. "The next boat leaves twelve days later, but steerage is completely booked. There's some space available on the one after that, though."

"And when does that boat sail?"

"Three weeks later," the clerk replied. Nikola told him he'd think it over and notify him of his decision, and went out into the sunlit street to review his financial situation. By quitting without notice he had deprived himself of any severance pay, so he had only his last two weeks' salary in his pocket. All of his savings had been used to purchase parts for his constructs in Strasbourg. By careful managing he knew he would be able to stretch what money he had to cover the railroad fare to the harbor, the boat fare, and leave enough to pay for a week's living expenses in America. He wanted very much to travel to Smiljan to say goodbye to his mother before leaving for America. However, if he had to wait a whole month before sailing, he would not have enough money to visit her and pay living expenses.

He decided that the best thing he could do would be to leave on the boat sailing the following Monday. In America he would soon make a fortune and be able to afford a trip back to Europe to see his mother. Meanwhile he would sell his books so that he could send her money for some little luxury. He went back into the steamship office and booked passage on the next boat.

CHAPTER 12

AFTER A WEEK of feverish activity, in which he just barely managed to complete all the necessary arrangements and accomplish all the many tasks he had set out to do, he was actually on his way to the railroad station the following Monday morning. In his wallet was his railroad ticket, his steamship ticket, and, when last counted, twenty four dollars—plenty for incidental expenses on the trip and living expenses for about a week in New York, he thought. Under his arm he carried all his belongings in one compact, tightly wrapped brown paper bundle. It contained his good suit, several shirts and changes of underwear, and three pairs of socks. He felt that he was well prepared for any emergency. He was mentally reviewing the contents of his parcel, checking his memory to make certain that he had not forgotten anything, when suddenly two men, approaching from the opposite direction, bumped into him, one on either side.

"Hey! Watch where you're going!" he exclaimed angrily. But he realized that the bumping had not been accidental when one of the men grabbed the bundle from under his arm and the other snatched the wallet from his hip pocket. Then they gave him a shove that sent him sprawling to the sidewalk, and ran off down the street without a word having been spoken or a sound uttered.

His first impulse was to run after them. He was taller than either of them and angry enough to beat up five men, let alone two! But he knew he didn't have much time. He reached for his watch—the watch his father had given him when he graduated from the institute ... It was gone. He didn't think he had time to chase the thieves and still make the train. He just couldn't miss it. He thought he had enough change in his pocket to pay the train fare, and once at the boat he could identify himself and have them confirm his passage at their Paris office. But if he missed the boat—well, he just wouldn't miss it. He began to run toward the station.

The train was just pulling out when he got there. He sprinted after it, caught up with it, and ran alongside it for several hundred yards until he spied one coach on which the doors had not yet been closed. Summoning all his remaining energy, he jumped, succeeded in catching hold of a metal bar on the side of the coach, and swung himself aboard.

The money in his pocket was enough to pay the train tare. The conductor was very sympathetic and suggested that Nikola have a telegram sent from one of the stations on the way.

"If you wire the steamship company in Paris they will telegraph the ship's officers so that they will allow you to board without question." Nikola agreed that it was a good idea, but he did not have enough money to send the telegram.

The ship's officers were considerably less sympathetic and much more skeptical than the conductor had been. They doubted his whole story. The implication that he was lying made Nikola very angry and when he was angry he invariably forgot to be either wise or tactful. He berated the ship's officers for their stupidity, which hardly endeared him. They shouted that there was no point to be gained by telegraphing the Paris office, for even if they were to receive confirmation of the fact that the reservation had been made and paid for by one Nikola Tesla, they would still not know that he was Nikola Tesla as he had on him no means of identification.

He suggested that they include in the telegram a request for a description of the man who had purchased the ticket. They scoffed at the idea that a busy clerk, who handled hundreds of reservations a day, would recall the appearance of a particular purchaser; but finally, to silence him and gain peace and time to go about their other business, they reluctantly complied with his request. The clerk did remember Nikola and sent an accurate description. Since there had been no other request for the reservation set aside in the name of Tesla, he was, at last, permitted to climb the steep gangplank. He was on his way to America!

He had hoped to meet some wealthy and influential American during the long journey—someone whom he could interest in the possibilities of his alternating current motor. But he realized that he could hardly expect a welcome on the upper decks. He could not expect to be treated like a celebrity, and an invitation to sit at the captain's table was not very likely. It was obvious, after a cursory glance about him, that there was no affluence among his many fellow steerage passengers. The only thing aboard the great liner that held any interest for him, therefore, was the engine room. He found his way down to the depths of the ship and spent most of his time watching the gigantic and complex mechanism.

As he sat on an overturned nail keg, observing the steady rise and fall of the great piston arms, he began to notice ways in which the construction might be improved. Hypnotized by the rhythm of the throbbing motor, he was oblivious alike to the almost intolerable heat and to the constant grumbling going on among the engine crew members. Actually, while he sat there, contemplating ways in which loss of power might be eliminated, a full sized mutiny was being planned all around him.

The first inkling he had that anything was amiss was given him when the second mate, accompanied by two big able bodied seamen, appeared without warning, on the narrow iron stairs that led topside and began laying about them with wildly swinging belaying pins. In an instant fists were flying, men were shouting, cursing, squealing in sudden pain. The mate swung his weapon at any head that showed itself. Nikola swung and landed an uppercut to the man's jaw and he went down without a sound. The engine crew, seeing that this footwork stranger was on their side, crouched behind him and gave him much verbal encouragement but little financial support. He ducked a blow that would have cracked his skull; everyone was hitting everyone else. Objects small enough to be picked up hurtled through the air; there was the sound of grunts and groans and shuffling feet. As suddenly as it had begun, it was ended by the appearance of a small army from up above. The men from the engine room were taken into custody, Nikola included. He explained that he was not one of them, and since his long, lean body and his aesthetic countenance seemed to confirm his statement, he was offered an apology and escorted to his quarters.

Thus it was that Nikola Tesla arrived in New York the following day, carrying no baggage but boasting a bandaged thumb, a cut on his right cheek, and a lump on his forehead which pushed his hat back on his head to a somewhat rakish and disreputable angle. He had exactly four cents in his pocket.

He experienced no sense of anxiety; on the contrary, his situation offered a challenge that he found exhilarating. Except for his damaged thumb, he had the full use of his hands— which he regarded with a new respect since they had knocked out two husky men the day before. He had the full use of his mind, and a letter in his pocket—the inner coat pocket—that would assure him of at least a night's lodging with a relative of Szigeti's. Tomorrow he would present himself to Mr. Edison and would be given a job immediately.

His cheerfulness received a slight setback when, upon inquiry, he learned that Szigeti's relative lived some thirty blocks away and that the bus fare was five cents. Well, a long walk would do him good, he thought. Give him a chance to stretch his legs and at the same time get a look at a considerable section of the city which he knew would be his home for a long time. All might have been well if he had not accidentally chosen to pass a section of lower Broadway where pushcart vendors sold food. The odors of cooking meat and cheese reminded him that he had had nothing to eat since the day before. Suddenly he was ravenous. He bought half a dozen pretzels for two cents, hoping they would allay his hunger until he reached his destination. But, as he walked, doubts assailed him. What it Szigeti's cousin was not home? Where could he stay? Where would he get anything to eat? He began walking faster. His one thought was to get to the address as quickly as possible. Had he not happened to hear loud cursing, expressed colorfully and fluently in his native Serbian tongue, he might never have looked into the open corrugated metal shed from which the sounds emerged. But the noise stopped him and he peered into the badly lighted little shop.

There he saw an elderly man bending over a small dynamo —one that might be used to operate a lathe. He held aloft a small electric light bulb attached to a long cord.

"Can't you find the trouble?" Nikola asked in Serbian, ducking his head in order to enter the low shed. The man straight tightened up as if he'd been jabbed by a hot needle. He turned and stared at Nikola.

"Who are you?" he asked. "Nobody speaks Serbian around here. That's why I can say what I please. Nobody understands it." Disconsolately he turned back to the dynamo. "If I only knew where to begin work on the confounded thing. I've tested all the connections—"

Tesla stepped closer and peered over the man's shoulder.

"Let me have a try," he urged. "I'm pretty good at fixing things."

"Why not?" The man stepped aside as Nikola removed his jacket and rolled up his sleeves.

He saw at once that the dynamo was very old and had received hard wear. It took only a few minutes for him to find out that many of the parts were worn beyond repair.

"Have you files and a drill handy?" he asked.

"Yes. This is a machine shop. I've got plenty of tools. It's just that I don't know the first thing about electricity. But I'm not alone in that—there's mighty few who do know anything about it."

"Is that so?" Nikola asked politely. "Where's the drill?"

"Over there, at the back of the shop. What you aimin' t'do?"

"Make new parts. The field coil is gone, for one thing and—"

"Make new parts! You know how t'do that?"

"Yes," Nikola answered simply and went to work. He worked for four solid hours before he was able to tell the little man to throw the switch. The dynamo whirred, caught, and steadied down to a soft, almost noiseless purr.

The little man looked at Nikola as if he were gazing upon a worker of miracles. "I can't thank you enough. How much do I owe you?"

Nikola was genuinely surprised. He had offered help at first only because the man had spoken Serbian. Then, as was usual with him, when he had seen the seriousness of the problem, the job itself had become a challenge. He had fixed the dynamo for the fun of overcoming obstacles.

"Could you treat me to a sandwich and a cup of coffee? Nikola asked. He had completely forgotten his hunger but now it was gnawing at his stomach.

"Don't talk like that," the man exclaimed indignantly. I'm no cheap sponger. You walk in here a complete strange and do a fine job of repair work. I don't want nobody to do nothing for me for nothing."

Nikola knew what he meant in spite of the somewhat con fusing grammar.

"I didn't mean to hurt your feelings," he said apologetically. "Just pay me whatever you think is fair."

The man drew out an old, worn wallet from his hip pocket. He scrutinized the contents thoughtfully for a moment, then pulled out two ten dollar bills and handed them to Nikola.

Twenty dollars! Twenty whole dollars

"That all right?" the man asked as Nikola stood staring at the bills in his hand.

"It's . . . isn't it too much?" he asked.

"Nonsense. I know I'm getting a bargain and if twenty seems fair, it's fine with me—just fine."

"It's just fine with me, too," Nikola said. He put the money in his pocket, bade his benefactor goodbye, and went out of the shop whistling tunelessly, his mind busy with thoughts of a thick, juicy steak, broiled onions, potato pancakes . . .

Thomas Alva Edison made a futile swipe at the unruly lock of white hair that persistently flopped down across his forehead, and handed the letter he had been reading to his wife. Mrs.

Edison had come down to her husband's headquarters on South

Fifth Avenue, to bring him some milk and hard boiled eggs, knowing he had worked all night and had probably forgotten to have breakfast. At first she glanced at the letter idly, then read it all the way through with increasing interest. "'I know two great men,'" Mrs. Edison read aloud. "'You are one of them. The other is the young man who will present this letter.' That's certainly high praise. Who wrote it? Is the man given to exaggerations of this sort?"

"Name's Batchellor," Edison said, "foreman of Production for Continental. Good man, knows his stuff. Knows men too. And, no, he's not given to exaggeration."

"Then hire this boy. Chief," Mrs. Edison urged. "It you had a really competent assistant, you might come home for dinner once in a while."

"I might just do that," Edison said. "On your way out you can ask this what's his name?—Nicholas Kessler—"

"Nikola Tesla," Mrs. Edison corrected, handing him Batchellor's letter of introduction.

"Tell him to come on in."

"Yes, Chief. And please behave yourself. Don't frighten the daylights out of the boy with your rough, tough, big boss act."

"What do you want me to do? Offer him a lollypop?"

He grinned as his wife turned toward him, ready to continue the argument. "All right, all right," he said hastily. "I won't frighten the little feller. I promise."

Mrs. Edison smiled, waved, and went out of the private office into the small waiting room. As she closed the door behind her, she nodded to Lucy Bogue who was typing at the secretary's desk, and turned to look at the only other occupant of the room. He was rising politely from the low chair in which he had been sitting, and to her startled eyes it seemed as if the rising process would never end. When at last he seemed to have reached his full height—six-feet-two—she found her voice.

"You are Mr. Tesla?" she asked.

"Yes, Madame."

"Mr. Edison will see you now. Excuse me," she added as she preceded him into the inner office and stepped aside to allow Nikola to enter.

Edison looked up toward the point in space where he expected to meet the Tesla boy's eyes. Instead, he found himself staring at the second button of Nikola's flowered vest. As he raised his eyes, the expression of incredulous amazement on his face was exactly what his wife had hoped for. She clapped a hand to her mouth, but did not quite succeed in stifling a giggle. Her husband drew his heavy eyebrows together in a deep, fierce frown as he glared at her for an instant. She closed the door quickly behind her, and Edison, still frowning, said gruffly:

"Sit down, Nicholas, sit down."

"Thank you, sir," Nikola said as he pulled a chair a little closer to the desk and sat. "The name is Tesla, sir, Nikola Tesla."

"That's quite a letter you sent in to me," Edison said. "Batchellor thinks highly of your work."

"He has seen what I can do."

"Hm. Yes. What else have you done—besides putting those governor gimmicks on some of Continental's dynamos?"

"I have perfected an alternating current, poly phase power—"

"Alternating current!"

"Yes, sir. I should like to explain—"

"Oh no you don't, Nicholas! Not to me, you won't. Fooling around with alternating current's just a waste of time. Nobody'll ever use it. Too dangerous! An alternating current high voltage wire gets loose, it could kill a man as quick as a bolt of lightning. Direct current's safe. Can't develop more'n one hundred and ten volts. Working on alternating current's a complete waste of time."

"I disagree/Mr. Edison, and I think I can convince you—"

"Not me, not me! Uh-uh Time's too valuable. If you want a job around here, you'd best forget all about alternating current."

"I can't do that, Mr. Edison."

"You do want a job here?"

"Yes, sir."

For a long moment the two men sat looking at each other in silence, each waiting for the other to break the deadlock.

Edison did not like what he saw. Most applicants for jobs held him in considerable awe. They stammered and blushed in their efforts to convince him of their willingness to work as an assistant to the Master.

The young man across the desk from him, on the other hand, seemed self-assured to the point of arrogance. Edison did not want to hire him. And yet he had to admit to himself, there were very, very few young men around who knew anything about electrical engineering. The blushers and the stammerers had not turned out too well, in spite of their eagerness and the deference they paid him. Then, too, if Edison disregarded Batchellor's letter and sent this young man packing, one of his competitors would grab him—and possibly make Edison look like a fool. He decided that it would be best to ignore his personal feeling.

"You know that all our machines and plants are operated on direct current?" he asked.

"Yes, Mr. Edison."

"Well, Nicholas, perhaps you can show us how we can save thousands of dollars on them, the way you did for Continental."

"Quite possibly, Mr. Edison."

Edison bit his lip. "You can start right away," he said, "and you may as well begin calling me 'Chief—like everybody else around here."

"Chief? Is there some significance—."

"Oh, you don't understand our American sense of humor," Edison exclaimed in exasperation.

"I prefer to call you 'Mr. Edison,' " Nikola said, rising, "and to be called Tesla. May I look over the plant now?"

Edison nodded speechlessly. He shook his shaggy head as if to clear it. As the door closed behind Nikola, he spoke out loud: "All I can say is, that boy better be as good as Batchellor says he is! He'd better be as good as he thinks he is or somebody'll murder him. I'll bet he's well heeled. Nobody could be that cocky unless he had a lot of money in his pockets."

Nikola had bought two new shirts, some underwear, a box of candy for the wife of Szigeti's cousin in appreciation of her hospitality. He had paid a week's rent in advance on a small room within two blocks of the Edison plant. Of the twenty dollars he had received the day before, about eight dollars remained in his new leather wallet.

CHAPTER 13

BY DOING EXACTLY what he had done in Paris for the Continental Edison Company, Nikola was able, after a few weeks, to come up with a plan whereby many thousands of dollars could be saved, both in the construction and in the operation of the Edison dynamos and motors. Edison, always interested in more economic operation, was intrigued by the suggestion, but not at all certain that it would work.

"Take a crack at it," he finally told Nikola. "Try it. There's fifty thousand dollars for you in it—if it works."

"How's the new man working out?" Mrs. Edison asked her husband a few days after Nikola had presented his plan.

"Don't know yet," Edison replied. "All I can say is—I've had a good many hardworking assistants in the past few years, but Tesla takes the cake. Works from ten in the morning till five the next morning, seven days a week—week in, week out. Don't see how he does it!"

"You're a fine one to talk, you are," Mrs. Edison exclaimed fondly.

Before Nikola had time to work out and test his ideas for increasing the efficiency of the Edison machines, he was given a rather spectacular opportunity to demonstrate his value and ability as an engineer.

The year before Nikola came to America, Edison had installed a minutemen lighting plant in the S.S. Oregon, the fastest and most luxurious passenger ship of the day. There had been no complaints. The Oregon had made several trips back and forth between New York and Southampton, and the electric light system had impressed and pleased both owners and passengers. But now, a day before the Oregon's scheduled sailing, both dynamos had failed. Edison found himself in serious difficulty. If the sailing had to be postponed—if there were cancellations of reservations—the steamship company might well sue Edison's company for heavy damages. Even if the great monetary loss were to be covered by insurance, the bad publicity resulting from the suit would take a heavy toll on profits for years to come. Naturally, Edison sent his most trusted team of workers to the ship at once.

They returned to explain the trouble. It would be impossible to remove the dynamos and install new ones; the old ones had to be repaired. But that could not be done without taking them to the shop, and that was impossible. As a last resort, Edison asked Nikola to go out to the ship to see if anything could be done. It was midafternoon The Oregon was scheduled to sail at eleven the following morning.

Nikola went out to take a look. The many hours he had spent on his long trip from Paris, watching the dynamos and visualizing the functioning of invisible parts, stood him in good stead. Within an hour Nikola had discovered the trouble— short circuits had caused some of the armature coils to burn out. He took off his jacket and rolled up his sleeves. He didn't have to ask for help; the engine crew volunteered to a man. They worked cheerfully all through the night. By four o'clock in the morning both dynamos were running as smoothly as when they had first been installed.

Returning to the shop, Nikola heard the clock in the City Hall tower strike five and he saw Edison coming out of the office. With him was Charles Batchellor, arrived the previous day from Paris. After enthusiastic greetings had been exchanged, Edison asked about the Oregon.

"The ship will leave on schedule, Mr. Edison," Nikola reported. "Both dynamos are operating."

As he went on into the office to write up his report, he heard Edison say, "That man's just as good as you said he was, Batchellor. In fact, he's even as good as he thinks he is!"

In the months that followed, Nikola worked on the improvements he had discussed with Edison. He designed twenty four new types of dynamos, eliminating the long core field magnets and substituting the far more efficient short cores. He invented some automatic speed controls that were registered at the Washington Patent Office in the name of the Edison Company. The Tesla magnets and controls increased the efficiency and reduced the cost of operating all the Edison dynamos then in use. Tests convinced Edison and his backers that Nikola had done everything that he had promised to accomplish.

At the end of that week Nikola found a ten dollar increase in his paycheck. Seething with anger, he wasted no time in seeking out Edison, whom he found in his office. Nikola held a crisp new ten dollar bill in one hand, his pay envelope in the other.

"Mr. Edison," he asked, "am I to understand that you wish me to wait ninety six years and eight weeks for the fifty thousand dollars?"

"Fifty thousand dollars? What fifty thousand dollars?"

"The fifty thousand dollars you promised me it I accomplished what I said I would. As you know, I have fulfilled my part of the agreement."

Edison threw back his head and laughed. "Oh, Tesla, Tesla!" he chuckled. "I told you you didn't understand the American sense of humor."

Nikola stared at him, unbelieving, shocked beyond words. He didn't trust himself to speak. Turning, he left the office, crossed the waiting room, entered his own office, and took his jacket and hat from the hat rack behind his desk. Putting them on, he left his office, closing the door behind him softly but with a certain finality. As he crossed the waiting room on his way out, the stenographer typing at the secretary's desk noticed that he tipped his hat politely to the closed door of Edison's office.

Edison's great and rapidly growing electrical empire had been built around his perfection of the incandescent electric light bulb. Although, when he patented it, it had been recognized as a revolutionary idea, there was no way in which bulbs could be sold in sufficient quantity to be commercially profitable, tor the simple reason that no homes, offices, or factories were wired for electricity. Candles, oil lamps, and gaslight were the sole sources of illumination. Therefore, in order to sell the bulbs, cities, towns, and individual home owners had to be "sold" on the idea of bringing electricity to their communities by means of local powerhouses. Edison did not invent the dynamo or the generator or the transformer. He did, however, develop their use in bringing electricity to the people and enabling them to purchase the use of it as a cost within their means. This was completely consistent with Edison's talent. He had never pretended to be a scientist. His great gift lay in his tremendous ability to translate the discoveries of other, more erudite, scientists into practical, commercial terms. It was natural that this gift should endear him to financiers and backers who had hitherto regarded inventors and scientists as impractical dreamers. It was also natural that Edison should incur the envy and jealousy of those scientists from whose original discoveries Edison made far more money than they did. And, when J. P. Morgan, a towering figure in the financial world of the period, threw his support behind Edison, he added to the ranks of Edison's enemies the many personal enemies and jealous, less successful financiers whose animosity he had aroused.

When Nikola—or, as he now preferred to be called, Tesla— had come to America, less than a year before he had talked to anyone and everyone who would listen about his alternating current, poly phase power system, and as a result succeeded only in creating the impression of being a dreamer. But there were very few skilled men in the field, and Nikola's miraculous achievement on board the Oregon as well as his improvements on the Edison direct current machines had been noted by watchful eyes.

When he tipped his hat in mocking farewell and walked out of the office of the Edison Company that spring morning in 1885, he found to his great surprise that he was walking into the outstretched welcoming arms of the rivals of Edison and Morgan. His services were in demand; financiers vied with each other in offers.

"At last!" he thought. It seemed as if the long awaited day had come when he could obtain financing to build the constructs needed to demonstrate his elaborate system. But he soon discovered that none of the groups bidding for his services were thinking in terms of so large a sum of money. One group of promoters, however, presented a suggestion that seemed to him to be both reasonable and realistic.

"Haven't you some other invention? One that would require less money to develop?" they asked. "If you do, then we could set up a corporation and provide the financing required. We would, of course, pay you generously and give you fifty per cent of the corporation's profits. Then, when the investors have received dividends and everyone is making money, it will be a simple matter for us to raise the larger amount that is needed for the big project."

So Tesla told them about his idea for an arc lamp for street lighting. It was a concept that had occurred to him soon after he had begun to work for Edison. In his mind he had fully worked out the details, of its operation. He had said nothing about it to Edison because he remembered only too well what had happened to him at the Continental Edison Company when he had spoken freely of ideas and improvements. They had been adopted without thanks or reward. He had not needed to put anything down on paper; there were no blueprints in existence. There could be no possible way in which the Edison Company might claim the idea, and it had the added appeal of being in direct competition with Edison's incandescent bulb. The promoters accepted the suggestion joyfully. The new corporation was formed and Tesla was presented with a beautifully engraved stock certificate entitling him to fifty shares of stock in the company.

Within a year the Tesla arc light was on the market. Given the same amount of current, the arc light had a far greater "throw" than the incandescent electric bulb, and therefore was tar better suited for street lighting and use in theaters where spotlights were required. The company prospered. But Tesla himself did not. His salary had ceased when he completed the work on the development of the light. He discovered too late that his 50 per cent interest in the company's profits did not entitle him to 50 per cent voting interest. Now that he had performed the services required of him, he was voted out of the company. When he tried to realize some cash by the sale of his engraved stock certificate, he soon learned that it was worthless. The company, at least according to its books, was reinvesting operating profits in the purchase of more materials, so it was obvious that no profits would be shown for several years. As for the company's backing him in the development of his alternating current system—"Out of the question!" "Ridiculous!" "Laughable!"

"Laughable." Was this another example of the American sense of humor? he wondered. He decided that there was nothing national about this particular kind of joke. He had not forgotten that it seemed to be just as amusing to the French owners of Continental Edison. He decided that it was more likely the promoters' sense of humor, but it was nonetheless a cruel and painful joke. What made it even more difficult was the fact that, in order to prevent him from suing for monies due him, the officers of the corporation spread the word around that he had been fired for incompetence. None of the other groups that had sought his services so eagerly the year before would now grant him an interview. For the first time in his life he was unable to get a job.

Assuming that his share of the profits from the arc light would surely be sufficient to take care of his modest personal needs, he had used his salary to purchase copper wire and other materials for which he thought he would be reimbursed when the company began to develop the alternating current motor. Now he was without reserve funds. Broke, jobless, and branded as erratic—a troublemaker and worse by his former colleagues _Nikola found himself in more desperate straits than he had ever before faced. His pride would not allow him to appeal to any relatives for help. He would not bring himself to write to Batchellor, who had returned to Paris. He began looking for work outside of his own field. He went to the little machine shop where, on his first day in America, he had helped the owner fix a broken dynamo, hoping that he might be given a job as a machinist or mechanic. The shop was closed, boarded up. A large For Sale sign was nailed to the boarding. Nikola turned away, disheartened. He decided to go back to his furnished room and try to sneak in without being seen by his landlady. He owed two weeks' rent and thought he had detected an unfriendly look in her eye when he left home that morning.

When he arrived at his address, he saw her. She was standing on the low, three step stoop. About to turn back in order to escape a scene with her, he suddenly realized that she was not looking in his direction. She was staring up the street and he looked to see what held her attention. In front of a building on Pearl Street, there was a long line of men extending from the building all the way to the corner. Nikola sauntered past his rooming house on the opposite side of the street and spoke to the last man in line.

"What's the lineup for?" he asked.

"Jobs," the man answered curtly.

"What kind?" Nikola persisted.

"They're gonna dig a ditch from here clear up into the open country past Forty second Street," the man replied. "Gonna lay some conduit for electric cables or something. They advertised for husky men."

"What's the pay?"

"Two dollars a day."

"I guess I'm husky enough," Nikola said and stepped onto the line.

CHAPTER 14

THE YEAR that followed was fully as important, if not actually more important, in the development of both Nikola Tesla the man and Tesla the scientist, as any year of his life—including the year in Budapest.

During the first few weeks a feeling of shame, bitterness, and self-pity only served to make him more fully aware of the stabbing pains at the backs of his legs, the steady, dull ache in his shoulder muscles. He thought of how shocked his mother would be if she knew. Or Professor Poeschl. Superman, genius, "star of the first magnitude"—swinging a pick ax alongside common day laborers! Nearly twenty years of study and schooling—the Real Gymnasium, the Higher Real Gymnasium, the institute, the university—and now twentieth assistant ditch digger!

Then, imperceptibly, his thinking began to change. Little by little he became more aware of the men working with him, and one day he realized, with considerable surprise, that he was no longer thinking of them as "common laborers." Most of the men were as new to this kind of work as he. It had been a bad year—bad for the farmers, the businessmen, the shop owners. The little man who worked six feet away from him had been a successful stockbroker. The stock market had behaved badly; his clients had lost their money—none of them could afford to buy in a selling market. He had a wife and two children. One man was a farmer who owned a big spread of land on Long Island. Bugs had killed the potato crop. A severe windstorm had blown down the alfalfa. He, too, had a wife and children. Another was a schoolteacher. He was married and they were expecting their first child. He was using his summer vacation to add to the tiny salary he received for teaching. Perhaps there was no such thing as "a common laborer."

The little man nearest him had a hard time digging the number of feet assigned to each man. As Nikola's muscles toughened and he found the work easier, he managed to trespass a foot or so onto the little man's territory. Nothing was said about it. Nikola was reminded of his first year at the Higher Real Gymnasium when a boy in the freehand drawing class seemed headed for the lowest marks in the class. The boy had happened to tell Nikola that if he got the lowest rating in any of his classes he'd lose his scholarship. Nikola was bad at freehand drawing and thoroughly disliked it. But he was not quite as inept as the other boy. Deliberately Nikola had drawn so badly that the other boy kept his scholarship. That had been before he had any serious idea of becoming a superman.

The second change that occurred in his thinking came with the sudden discovery that the rhythmic swinging of the pick no longer required any concentration. He found that his mind was clearer and more open to ideas than it had been since that productive year in Paris and Strasbourg. Freed of the pressure of mental work, his mind seemed to respond to the months of rest. New plans, new projects crowded into it.

Filling the vacuum, he thought with amusement: I really should write to old Poeschi to tell him of the new ingredient: Billiards, uninteresting friends, poetry, and now ditch digging.

He suddenly became aware of the fact that for the past five years his mind had been fully occupied with the defense of his alternating current system. Now he allowed himself to think of things that he had filed away in his mental filing cabinet. It was at this time that he began to give serious consideration to a theory that had been clamoring for his attention—like a child tugging at his father's coattails. It was the growing conviction that electric current waves and sound waves were, or could be, related. If this were true, it would be possible to transmit sound through the air without wires.

He had perfected the amplifier on his very first job for the telephone company in Budapest. He would have to work on further sensitizing the receiver, or earphone, and he would have to do a great deal of experimentation in order to determine the earth's magnetic charge. But as he thought about it day after day, swinging his pick in the heat of a New York summer, the more convinced he was that it could be done. If he was right, his visualization showed him that a ground wire, an aerial— to act as magnified ears and select the impulses transmitted to it electrically—would complete a circuit. He could not, without actual laboratory experiments, determine the manner in which the receiver would select these impulses, but he envisioned a complete method of broadcasting without wires. Once having worked it out, he put it aside and opened his mind to the consideration of linking electric, or electronic, wavelengths with light waves. It this could be done, it would be possible to transmit images! It sounded fantastic, he knew, and yet, had he not always been able to materalize an image, even of a mathematical formula written on a blackboard? A Frenchman named Daguerre had shown how you could throw an image onto a sensitized surface, such as tin, and record it with accuracy. A device that could break up the image into its component parts would be necessary. Then the light waves could reassemble these parts by transmission through a lens.

The days sped by. The pickax no longer scraped and tore at his callused hands. He was no longer aware of its weight as he swung it hour after hour. The half hour lunch periods were pleasant too. He found that he could talk about his ideas to the men as they sat munching sandwiches from their tin lunchboxes. What if they didn't understand? They were a far more polite audience than the executives at Continental Edison had been. They listened. They even asked questions. He found himself talking as he had never been able to talk before. And, in turn, he learned to listen as he had never listened in his whole life. He found that the problems of the men around him held his interest and that, strangely enough, considering their problems seemed to lighten his own. The summer was over before he knew it.

It was very early on a morning in September, 1887, that the little man who worked six feet away from him in the ditch approached him as they were rolling up their jackets and placing them in a big green locked box, before climbing down into the ditch.

"I've got a favor to ask of you," the little man said shyly.

"I've ... well, I hope you won't think I've butted in where I'm not wanted but—well, I may as well come out with it. I've made an appointment with a—a sort of friend of mine to meet you."

"Meet me?" Nikola exclaimed. "Why?"

"Well," the little man answered, squirming uncomfortably under Nikola's penetrating stare, "you see, when I had my own brokerage office, I knew people—well, this man, Mr. Brown, he always had lots of money and he always liked to gamble in the more speculative stocks. I thought, maybe, if you'd go with me and talk to him, the way you talk to us during lunch hour, well, he might get interested ... It couldn't do any harm, could it? I mean, if you were to tell him about this alternating current thing and what it could do toward bringing down the cost of living—well, I mean, what've you got to lose?"

Nikola stared at the little man in amazement. For the first time in his life he felt an emotion he could not analyze. He felt moisture gathering in his eyes.

"Of course, I'll go. Gladly and gratefully," he said simply. "When is the appointment?"

"Tomorrow."

"Saturday?"

"Yes, Mr. Brown said he'd give up his usual stroll in the park and come to his office. He said you sounded kind of like a nut, but sometimes things that sounded nutty turned out better than things that sounded foolproof and ironclad."

The two men walked over to the side of the ditch and the little man started climbing down the short ladder leading to the bottom. Standing on the lowest rung, he looked up at Nikola towering above him.

"Just one more thing," he said. "Don't tell him anything about this or how we met or anything. He was my biggest customer. I never went to him for help when things went sour. I don't want him to know—he thinks I've retired."

Nikola, laughed. "Of course, I shan't tell him. We're just a couple of retired disgruntlement who happened to meet at Sherry's and began discussing the many advantages of the poly phase alternating current power system!"

Still laughing, he ignored the ladder and sprang down into the ditch. "You know something?" he said. "I don't even know your name. We've always called you 'Mac.' "

"McCollum," the little man said. "I know that yours is Tesla, isn't it?"

"Nikola Tesla. I'm glad to meet you, Mr. McCollum."

He held out his huge right hand and the little man took it, grinning as they formally shook hands.

Tesla often thought that neither Shakespeare nor Goethe— nor, for that matter, any author whom he respected—could have written the scene that took place the following morning. It would have seemed to them too contrived, too improbable, and utterly unbelievable.

Tesla and McCollum met on the sidewalk and together climbed the worn wooden steps of an old building to the large, second floor offices of the Western Union Telegraph Company. There was no receptionist, or anyone in sight, but a hearty voice called out to them:

"Come right in, McCollum."

The little man led the way toward a glass partitioned office. On the glass Nikola read the words, A. K. Brown, Exec. Vice Pres

Mr. Brown listened attentively to Tesla's description of the difference between alternating and direct current. Then he held up one well-manicured hand.

"Excuse me for interrupting, Mr. Tesla," he said, "but there's a friend of mine I'd like to have hear this. I asked him to stand by for a phone call. Before I called, I wanted to get an idea of what it was all about."

"And decide whether or not I was a 'nut'? Tesla asked, smiling.

Mr. Brown grinned. "Exactly," he admitted. "Now my friend Werber knows a great deal more about such things than I do. Also, he has a great deal more liquid cash than I have, since he's just sold out a chain of small shops he owned. I don't want you to have to go over the whole thing twice."

"Twice!" Tesla echoed. "I've been over it a thousand times and I'd gladly repeat it a thousand more!" Mr. Brown smiled and picked up the telephone.

While they were waiting for Mr. Werber, Tesla told Mr. Brown something of his background. When they heard footsteps on the stairs, Mr. Brown called out, "In here, Albert."

The footsteps drew nearer. The door opened. Mr. Albert Werber stood in the doorway. He stared at Nikola in surprise. Tesla looked at him and gasped—the man whose dynamo he had fixed! Mr. Werber was the first to recover from his surprise.

"Aha!" he exclaimed. "It's my good Samaritan. You can stop worrying about this man's being a nut, A.K. I'm willing to state right now in front of witnesses that a man who can doctor a sick dynamo the way this man fixed mine is no nut! Now let's hear about this plan of yours, Tesla. What's it all about?"

Tesla hesitated a moment before answering. "Forgive me it I do you a grave injustice, but it is perhaps best if I assume that you gentlemen understand little or nothing of the difficulties under which Mr. Edison's present day powerhouses now operate."

"That will be no injustice, Mr. Tesla," Mr. Brown replied, smiling. "At least insofar as I am concerned. I could hardly know less."

The others nodded and echoed Mr. Brown's protestations of innocence and Tesla smiled and began his explanation.

"Electricity is generated, either by water power or fire, in powerhouses by small dynamos. The current is distributed to customers through copper conductors laid in conduits under the streets. But a great deal of the electrical energy fed into the conductors does not arrive at the tar end of the line because it is converted along the route into useless—even dangerous— heat by the resistance of the conductors."

The men nodded to show that they were able to follow his explanation thus far, and Tesla continued:

"Electrical energy is composed of two component parts: Current—or the amount of electricity—and voltage, which is the pressure under which the current is moved. Resistance and heat losses affect the current regardless of the voltage. If the amount of current carried by a wire is doubled, the heat losses are quadrupled, for the loss is always the square of the increase. Naturally, this limits the amount of current that can be loaded onto the conductors."

He paused for a moment to examine the faces of his listeners. They were following his every word with intense interest.

"Just to make things a little more complicated," Tesla went on, "while the voltage doesn't increase or decrease the resistance loss, an increase in resistance loss does create a loss of voltage. As a result, direct current, as it's now generated in Mr. Edison's powerhouses, can serve only an area of approximately one square mile. You see what that means? It means that, to serve a large city, one would have to build a powerhouse every square mile. The little towns and villages all over this big country present an even greater problem. Powerhouses cost money. Copper wire costs money when it's bought by the mile! But, with Mr. Edison's direct current, many powerhouses and many, many miles of cable are required because there's no way—with direct current—of stepping up or transforming an electric current. The voltage remains fixed. The wires can carry only their limited load.

"Gentlemen, is it any wonder that people laugh when we tell them that electricity will one day be America's greatest source of light and power? 'A dream—a crazy dream!' they say, 'Electricity will never take the place of gaslight and whale oil!' And the sad thing is that they are right! The farmers, the working people in the small towns—they will never know the wonders of electricity ... not as long as people must depend on direct current!"

The men looked at each other, Mr. Brown smiled. "And with your alternating current, Mr. Tesla, will all the world's problems be solved?"

Suddenly Tesla realized that he had been preaching and that he must have sounded very pompous to his important listeners. He grinned boyishly.

"Perhaps not all of them, Mr. Brown," he admitted. "The world may still be troubled by a few problems, even if my alternating current system is accepted. But there will be fewer problems. You see, I have invented transformers—which are simple coils of wire wound around an iron core—and they can be used to step up the voltage and, at the same time, reduce the current in direct proportion so that greater amounts of energy can be sent through those same wires without creating resistance and heat loss."

"You mean that with your system a very small copper wire can carry a greater load than it could with direct current?" Werber asked.

"Exactly," Tesla answered, his dark eyes shining with excitement. "It can carry a thousand times the current! That means it can carry great currents vast distances without great expense —electricity need no longer be limited to local use. It means that it can be freed ..."

Five hours later Mr. Brown persuaded his attorney to leave his weekend guests and come over to the office. A public stenographer was prevailed upon to come and take dictation, at double time rates because it was Saturday. By seven o'clock that evening contracts had been drawn up and signed. The Tesla Electric Company had been formed. On Monday, fifty thousand dollars would be deposited in an account set up in the name of the new corporation. Tesla was to find a location for a laboratory that would meet his own needs and office space and demonstration rooms. It was agreed that the first monies taken in by the new company would be used to reimburse the two investors, and any others they might interest in the venture. After this money had been paid back, the investors would get 50 per cent of the annual profits and Tesla would receive the same amount. Mr. McCollum, in return for having brought the Tesla project to them, would receive a "finder's fee," which meant that he would receive a generous share of the profits without having to put up any money.

When at last the papers were all signed, Mr. Werber stood up and stretched. "Do you realize what all this means, A.K..?" he asked. "It means we've got hold of the biggest thing since the flood."

Tesla, more than slightly dazed by the whirlwind speed of the events of the past few hours, thought to himself: How can he—how can anyone know what it means? From ditch digger to officer of a corporation in less than twenty four hours. Everything I've hoped for—my own lab ... His attention suddenly focused on what Mr. Werber was saying.

"__and that's the trouble with the Edison dynamos. With direct current you can only service an area of about one square mile. The Edison bulbs operate on one hundred and ten volts. They build a powerhouse in the area they plan to service. The wires carry one hundred and twenty volts to compensate for the loss of voltage caused by the resistance in the copper con doctors. So what happens? The people living a block or two away from the powerhouse get an excess of voltage, so their bulbs burn out quicker than they should. Those living at the mile wide perimeter get only about ninety volts, so they com plain that they don't get enough light to read by. With Tesla's setup, on the other hand, cables carrying one hundred thousand or a million volts can be led right into a powerhouse, which can then service an area covering hundreds of miles instead of one, without the loss of a single volt in transmission! I tell you, A.K., this man has released the sleeping giant called electricity! He's cut the bonds that tied it to the powerhouse. He's set it free!"

The tiger, Tesla thought, the tiger I used to dream of letting out of its cage. The tiger that only I could tame.

The whirlwind continued on its dizzying course. On Monday morning Tesla found a building large enough to suit his needs. It was located on South Fifth Avenue, less than three blocks from Edison's headquarters. The Battle of the Titans was on!

Building of the constructs got under way at once. Again, no blueprints were needed. Tesla recalled every dimension of each part for the complicated machines. It was only a matter of weeks before models of dynamos, motors, transformers, regulators, and every other unit of the elaborate poly phase alternating current power plant were completed. As fast as they were finished, the inventions were registered in the Patent Office. When the last one was registered, Tesla applied for a single patent that covered the entire operation. The Patent Office wrote stating that, whereas each and every one of the inventions was original, they could not grant one overall patent and that they would issue the separate patents immediately upon receipt of the applications.

When announcements began to appear in the engineering trade journals of twenty five patents issued in quick succession to a man whose name was known to only a few individuals, the entire electrical engineering profession was stunned. The significance and the simplicity of Tesla's revolutionary discoveries were immediately apparent. These discoveries were epoch making! They would certainly create tremendous activity—a new field, new jobs, new opportunities for every electrical engineer.

When Tesla received an invitation in May, 1888, to speak before the American Institute of Electrical Engineers, he knew that his gift to the world for the betterment of mankind had been recognized. To be able to speak on a subject so dear to him seemed to be the opportunity he had waited for all these years. It was a chance to tell the whole world of the infinite and breathtaking possibilities of the power system that had now progressed from a "visualization" in his mind, and his mind alone, to a firm and definite reality. The speech he wrote was simple and yet majestic. The several hundred engineers who packed the auditorium felt themselves present at an awe inspiring moment in the history of the civilized world. At the conclusion of the lecture there was a long moment of complete silence. Then, as one, the entire audience rose to its feet to give a standing vote of confidence and pay homage to a man deemed by all present to be the outstanding inventor in the electrical field.

And now he. Brown, and Werber were besieged by offers of additional financing as well as promotional plans for the manufacture of the new machines. Tesla knew that a great deal of money was to be made by the manufacture and sale of motors and dynamos operating on alternating current. There were none on the market and, unless he leased his patents, he was the only one permitted to make and sell them. Yet alternating current, which the engineering world had finally recognized as more powerful and less expensive than direct current, could not be furnished except by means of his patented machines. In fairness to Brown and Werber and McCollum, he felt that he could not dismiss lightly the moneymaking opportunities thus offered, but he was not interested in the manufacture of machines and tools. He wanted to be free to continue his experiments, improve the existing machines, and develop new ones. He wanted, also, to devote time to training assistants whom he could call upon to help him develop the broadcasting system he had visualized while ditch digging.

He was wrestling with this problem when he received a letter from an engineer named George Westinghouse. The letter stated that its writer had read about the speech at the Association meeting and had sent for a copy thereof. After reading it and studying its contents, the writer requested an interview with Mr. Tesla, and would appreciate being given an opportunity to study the models and constructs in operation.

Nikola had heard of George Westinghouse. His company, the Westinghouse Electric Company, was the only one that had refused to be absorbed by the overgrowing Edison empire, which had gobbled up all other competitors, small and large, and had merged them into the company now known as the Edison General Electric Company. Tesla wrote at once, inviting Mr. Westinghouse to visit the laboratory and demonstration rooms on South Fifth Avenue at his very earliest convenience.

Westinghouse, always a man to act quickly, came to New York from Pittsburgh a few days later and, without stopping to check into a hotel, came directly from the station to the Tesla Electric Company building. Never were two men so alike mentally and in their ability to see into the vast panorama of the future, yet so completely unlike physically. Westinghouse was short, stocky, with a graying blonde Vandyke beard and a gruff, hearty voice; Tesla was tall, clean shaven, with his dark hair parted in the middle and brushed back from his forehead. His voice was seldom raised above a quiet conversational tone. Each man took an instant liking to the other. It was a great treat for Tesla to be able to show off his machines to someone whose mind leaped ahead to their possibilities, without the need for laborious and painstaking explanations.

Westinghouse found complete confirmation of what he had expected to find: a scientist of complete integrity whose inventions would inevitably be worth a fortune. He decided then and there that there was no point in stalling for time or fencing for terms.

"I will give you one million dollars for all your alternating current patents, plus royalty," he blurted out.

A million dollars! Tesla had never dreamed of receiving so much money all at one time. A million dollars. He could make people rich and still have enough to continue his experiments. He was as electrified as if one of his own high tension wires had touched his hand. But not in vain had he learned self-discipline, not in vain those hours of chess in which a glint in the eye would foretell a move to an alert opponent. "If you will make the royalty one dollar per horsepower used, I shall accept the offer," he said.

"A million cash, a dollar a horsepower royalty," Westinghouse repeated.

"That is acceptable," Tesla said quietly.

"Sold," Westinghouse said and stuck out his hand. As Tesla grasped it firmly, Westinghouse added, "You will receive a check and a contract in a few days."

The two men walked toward the door together. Westinghouse picked up his suitcase.

"By the way," he asked, turning at the threshold, "just how many patents are there?"

"There are now forty," Tesla replied.

"I haven't done so badly," Westinghouse said, grinning broadly. "That's only twenty five thousand dollars per patent. Not bad. Not bad at all!"

He waved cheerfully with his free hand and strode out the door and down the street.

CHAPTER 15

UPON RECEIPT of so large a sum of money, it would have been understandable if Tesla, now only thirty three, had relaxed, taken a vacation, or become a playboy. None of these things happened. He paid five hundred thousand dollars—half the total—to Mr. Brown and Mr. Werber, in accordance with their agreement, and was pleased by the thought that little Mr. McCollum would benefit to a handsome degree. After paying this obligation and reimbursing them for all monies that they had spent on the building of the constructs, he was left with something less than four hundred thousand dollars. No mean sum! he thought—particularly when it would be augmented at the end of a year by the royalty arrangement.

At last he was in a position to realize his dreams. He sent substantial sums to his mother and sisters. The balance he began to spend on new and expensive materials required for his experimentation on radio and wireless transmission. He engaged secretaries so that he might get down on paper much of the information that he had kept locked in his mental file, and he offered prizes and scholarships to promising students at M.I.T. and Harvard and Columbia, with the intention of obtaining from their number a staff of highly trained, intelligent assistants.

He turned down without a second thought offers to lecture to university audiences and engineering associations both in America and abroad. He had no more desire to become a public figure than he had to become a manufacturer or a business tycoon. Not that he was unaware of what such recognition and worldly success would mean. He was no absentminded professor, living only in some abstract realm of science. On the contrary, he was intoxicated by the idea that so many choices were open to him. He felt that he had come a long way toward his boyhood goal of disciplining his mind and body to such an extent that he could make both do his bidding. With money and time it seemed to him that there was nothing to prevent his becoming the greatest scientist the world had ever known. There were so many things he knew that no one else had ever dreamed of! He wanted to give all these ideas—these unborn brain children—to the world as quickly as possible. He was still a young man and a lifetime stretched before him—but it was only one lifetime, and there was so much to be done.

There was the microphone and loudspeaker that he had worked on as a young man with the telephone company in Budapest. He was sure that he could perfect a means of transmitting messages without wires. He also felt that he could develop a means of transmitting pictures, without wires, by use of electronic impulses. And then there was the relationship of electric current to light waves. He was convinced that waves of current could be transformed into waves of light that could be used for illumination far more effectively and economically than by Edison's incandescent bulb.

But first of all—before he could settle down to work on any of the countless projects he had in mind—he felt obliged to see that his alternating current system was given to the world as quickly as possible. Therefore, when George Westinghouse asked him to leave his own laboratory and come to the Westinghouse plant in Pittsburgh to supervise the manufacture of the dynamos and transformers and motors needed for the practical application and installation of the new system, Tesla felt that this was an obligation that took precedence over everything else.

Things did not go well in Pittsburgh. All the models and constructs that Tesla had demonstrated to Westinghouse in the laboratory had been designed to operate with a current of 60 cycles. When he arrived at the Westinghouse plant, he discovered that the engineers in charge of the Tesla motor project had decided that a higher frequency of 133 cycles would produce a greater efficiency of operation. They were wrong. He had spent years experimenting with varying frequencies and knew that, while there was a saving in the amount of iron required at the higher frequencies, the resultant drop in efficiency ate up that saving. On the other hand, he had discovered that at frequencies below 60 the efficiency increased but the cost of materials did too, because a great deal more iron was needed.

Undoubtedly this difference of opinion could have been worked out amicably had it not been for the disparaging and somewhat patronizing attitude of the engineers. They antagonized Tesla by their very obvious belief that, while he was undoubtedly a great inventor, he was assured of his money and had no reason to consider as seriously as they the need for commercially profitable manufacture and installation of his equipment. As weeks passed in futile and evermore bitter argument, it became evident that no decisions could or would be made without causing embarrassment for his friend George Westinghouse, who was compelled to take sides; and Tesla knew that it would be greatly to everyone's disadvantage if he decided against his own engineers and foremen, who were going to have to do the actual work of making and selling the Tesla motors and dynamos.

Having sized up the situation and found it most unsatisfactory, Tesla went to Westinghouse. "I've got to get back to my lab," he said. "I don't think I'm really needed here and I've no reliable assistants in New York who can carry on there while I'm away."

Westinghouse looked at him, his piercing blue eyes seeming to penetrate Tesla's mild mannered bluff.

"I think I need you, Tesla," he answered, his fingers pulling at his bushy beard. "Perhaps I shouldn't have asked you to come here without salary. Perhaps I—"

"You know it isn't that, Westinghouse," Tesla interrupted. "You must know that the most important thing in my life is the alternating current system. I want only to get it in use as quickly and as economically as possible. But you have Cronson and Krauss and the others. They, too, want the same thing. I am not needed—"

It was Westinghouse's turn to interrupt. "I'll give you two thousand a month and a third of the net profits it you'll stay on and direct the work," he said with characteristic decisiveness.

"Twenty four thousand dollars a year!" Tesla could hardly believe his ears. "You can't mean that! You'll get just as much of my enthusiasm and my help for nothing. It's unbelievably generous—"

"You'll stay?"

"I can't accept the offer. It wouldn't be fair to those who have invested in me. It wouldn't be right to keep from the world the other things I'm working on. I—"

"What if I were to throw in ... a laboratory of your own?"

"My own lab! It is a fabulous offer, Westinghouse! I cannot thank you enough for having made it. It proves that there is at least one other person besides myself with complete confidence in my ability. But the answer must still be no."

"For heaven's sake, why?" Westinghouse exclaimed. He arose from the desk chair in which he'd been sitting and came around to Tesla. "How can you be so sure that—"

Tesla smiled down at him.

"It wouldn't work. Believe me, it wouldn't! For one thing, there would be friction—"

"Never! I'd see to it—"

"Westinghouse," Tesla interrupted, "when you buy a new hat, how do you go about it?"

"Hat? What's that got to do with—"

"Humor me. This is a demonstration. How do you go about buying yourself a new hat?"

"I go to a hat shop and try on hats until I find one that fits and—"

"Exactly! The Thomas A. Edison method! Trial and error. Waste of time."

"Oh, come now," Westinghouse exclaimed impatiently, "And just exactly how would the great Nikola Tesla——"

Tesla laughed. "You see? I have already proved half my point. You are irritated because you think I am being superior. Well, I must always irritate people because I know my way is superior! For nearly thirty years I have trained my mind to do my bidding. It would be too bad if, by this time, it were not superior to those without such training.

"You want to know how Tesla would buy a hat? I'll tell you. There on your desk is a steel tape measure. Without even closing my eyes, I visualize it held tightly around my head. In my mind I can see the markings on the tape—twenty-two and nineteen thirty-second inches. That means I could not wear a hat that is marked 'seven and a quarter.' I should have to get that size 'seven and five eights'. And now will you be so kind as to check my measurements?"

"No!" Westinghouse exploded. "I'll not make a fool of myself. You've measured your head size at some other time, although why you'd want to—"

Tesla threw back his head and laughed.

"When I was a boy in school," he said when he could speak, "my teachers accused me of cheating, just as you have accused me now! They believed I memorized the answers in the back of the book. I proved my innocence. With your help I'll do it again. I've never used a tape measure Come, see if I am right."

Sheepishly Westinghouse took the little steel tape and bent it around Tesla's head. "Of course, you're right," he said. "To the dot. You give me your word, you've never measured your head before or been told the dimensions?"

"I give you my word."

Westinghouse mumbled something in his beard. He lit a fat cigar and began puffing it vigorously as he paced from one side of his office to the other. Tesla watched him, his eyes twinkling quizzically, but he said nothing. After several swallowtail round trips, Westinghouse looked up at his friend and suddenly his even white teeth showed between his handlebar mustaches and his beard as he grinned boyishly.

"I get your point," he said. "That gift of yours—or trick or whatever it is—can be pretty all-fired annoying! Still I say, it's not a good enough reason to justify your refusal to—"

"Your guess is a good one. There are at least two other reasons," Tesla admitted. "In the first place, I can no longer work happily as part of an organization. My experience with the telegraph company in Budapest and later with the Paris Edison Company and again in Edison's New York plant have all left their mark. I'm afraid I'd soon begin to resent having my brains picked by my boss and I'd completely forget that I myself was one of the bosses."

Westinghouse nodded. "I understand that feeling. Had it myself."

"And the most important reason is that I've planned so full a schedule for myself. If I were here, I should feel that it was only right that problems of the plant would have first call upon my time; but I know that I want to work without interruption. You see, I want to try to correlate light waves with electric current waves. I have a feeling that finding the answer will mean a great deal to the world—and not only in the field of illumination. Then I want to work on the improvement of the transmission of sound over wires. When that is accomplished, I wish to work on the transmission of sound without wires. Then images first with wires, then without. I realize how fantastic this sounds, but I know that either the very earth carries an electric charge or else it is an excellent conductor. In either case, it should be possible to use it to transmit sounds and images through the electrically charged air we breathe. I must learn of these things, Westinghouse. An exciting future lies before me. I am impatient to begin."

"I think I should be, too, if I could see—even dimly and in the far off future—the realization of dreams like yours. I'll be sorry to lose you, but . . . best of luck to you,"

"Thanks," Tesla said softly. "If you should need my help on anything in connection with the building or operation of the dynamos and motors, you have only to telegraph. If necessary, I'll be on the next train. Nothing must stop or delay the electrification of the United States."

The two scientists shook hands with considerable solemnity. Then, once again, Tesla smiled.

"Let your men go on experimenting with the one hundred and thirty three frequency they're so sure of. And if that doesn't work, let them go shopping for other sizes. But I'm willing to wager a dinner at the Waldorf-Astoria that, in the end, they'll discover that the hat most becoming to the Tesla motor is size sixty!"

CHAPTER 16

THERE WAS ANOTHER REASON for Tesla's leaving Pittsburgh—a reason he did not disclose to Westinghouse, possibly because he was not fully aware of it himself. He liked many things about the older man and they might easily have become close friends. In spite of the fact that his year of ditch digging had shown Tesla the warmth and pleasures that friendship offered, he still felt that the distraction would be too great a price to pay. Although he was a young man, he had glimpsed an illimitable vision. There was endless work to be done, important discoveries to be made, which would benefit mankind and make life easier for all those who had to work for a living—and he regarded this as an almost sacred duty. Friendships would only use up his precious time, the money that he would have spent on entertaining could be used for the purchase of new materials and the hiring of assistants.

When, on that early evening in the wooded park in Budapest, the vision of the rotating magnetic field had come to him, it had brought with it an odd sense of understanding the universe. He had viewed the whole cosmos as a symphony of alternating current, and to Tesla it had seemed that the harmonies could be explained if they were considered as being played on a scale of electrical vibrations of many octaves. At the lower end of the scale was the single note—the 60-cycle-per-second alternating current. Somewhere in the higher octaves was visible light, with its frequency of billions of cycles per second. He wanted to explore the region of electrical vibration that lay between these two. If the first and most rudimentary of his discoveries could result in the magnificent poly phase alternating current motor, what might not be awaiting discovery in the higher frequencies! He wanted to build a machine that would produce electrical vibrations in all frequencies. If he succeeded, he would be in a position to study the characteristics of each wavelength and make comparative deductions.

Remembering the treatment that had been accorded him by the Paris Edison Company, Tesla was determined that no one who worked for him would be exploited. He felt that he had no need to pick anyone else's brain. His own had pointed the way to more work in the next half century than could possibly be accomplished by anyone with a mind less disciplined than his. As a result he did not hire physicists or chemists or mathematicians as assistants. He engaged only artisans and mechanics who could build or make the machines and instruments according to the specifications he gave.

None of these "assistants" knew the nature of the project they were working on. They only knew the function of the particular part on which they were working. Nor was any one of them ever given a blueprint to work from. Tesla supplied the necessary dimensions and specifications from the prodigious mental filing cabinet that he had maintained ever since his boyhood days in the library at Go spic

He had many reasons to be thankful for that filing cabinet at this particular time, for he very soon discovered—as many other great scientists were later to discover—that light waves, electric current, and energy were all closely interrelated. Thus, while he was working on the production of a heatless light, he might easily come upon a scientific truth pertaining to the transmission of sound. He never permitted this unexpected finding to distract him from the experiment on which he was concentrating. On the other hand, he did not want to lose or forget the irrelevant information. So he "filed" it in his mind and could draw upon it whenever he got around to working on the experiment to which that particular information pertained.

Neither the scientists of his own era nor those who succeeded him have been able to give an explanation for the amazing rapidity with which Nikola worked. Nor have they been able to explain how one man could have so many inventions credited to him. He was able to work on four or five inventions simultaneously, even though they might concern fields that were seemingly wholly unrelated.

One of the many projects that interested Tesla at this time was the production of light by a simpler, less wasteful and expensive method than incandescence. In order to test his theory he built rotary alternating current dynamos with as many as three hundred eighty four magnetic poles. With these he was able to generate currents up to 10,000 cycles per second! Although he had engaged upon this venture with the idea of approximating more closely the frequency of light waves, he discovered incidentally that these high frequency currents produced even more efficient power transmission than his own very successful 60cycle poly phase system. He therefore worked on the two parallel experiments simultaneously, both requiring a device that would raise and lower the voltage of the currents used.

The high frequency current transformers that Nikola designed and had his workers execute in his laboratory proved to be spectacularly successful. They contained no iron. They were air core transformers and consisted of primary and secondary coils. With these "Tesla coils" he found it possible to produce waves by the spark discharge of an induction coil and absorb them back from space and change them to a small spark at some distance from the coils. Within a matter of weeks, with the increased voltages he could now obtain, he could produce flaming discharges that leaped across the width of the laboratory. Working as he was with such tremendously high voltages, it was inevitable that he should encounter difficulty in insulating his apparatus. He decided that if the apparatus itself were to be immersed in oil and all air kept from the coils, the entire machine would be heat and fire resistant This minor experiment, engaged in only because he did not want to be delayed in his major experiment, resulted in the method of insulation that was adopted by scientists and electricians everywhere. Tesla never thought of patenting it, nor did he ever derive any income from it though it proved to be of tremendous commercial value.

For the first time in his life, Tesla was free to work as he had for so long imagined himself working. Freed from financial worries and from all distracting personality differences, his mind worked as smoothly and quickly as any of the pieces of apparatus in his laboratory. Without frictionless his ideas were released in a constant, uninterrupted flow. The results were almost beyond belief. There was no such thing as the impossible. What seemed impossible became a challenge to be tackled at once.

When, for instance, he realized that there was a limit above which the use of rotary generators of high frequency currents was not practicable, he determined to develop a different type of generator. In rotary dynamos, current is generated by moving a wire in a circle past a number of magnetic poles in succession. Tesla decided to try moving the wire back and forth with an oscillating motion in front of a single magnetic pole. No one had ever succeeded in producing a practical, workable, reciprocating dynamo. A number of engineers who had tried declared that it was impossible. That was the only challenge Tesla required. He got to work on it at once. He built a six cylinder engine without valves that could be operated by compressed air or steam. It was supplied with ports—like a two cycle marine engine. A rod extended from the piston through the cylinder head at either end and at each end of the rods was attached a flat coil of wire, which was caused to move back and forth through the field of an electromagnet by the reciprocating action of the piston. The magnetic field, because of its cushioning effect, served as a flywheel.

Tesla obtained a speed of twenty thousand oscillations per minute with this device but—far more important—a degree of steadiness and constancy of operation that had never before been achieved. So amazingly constant was the operation of this "impossible" motor that Tesla suggested to his assistants and workers that it could well be made to serve as a timekeeper. He pointed out that by using synchronized motors, geared down to the proper extent, accurate time could be recorded wherever alternating current was in use.

This suggestion undoubtedly reached at least one pair of alert ears, for it proved to be the foundation on which rests the production of electric clocks. Tesla, however, having satisfied himself by achieving the "impossible," had no further interest in it and, of course, made no attempt to patent the principles evolved. Feeling that he had wasted precious time, he told himself that in the future he must discipline himself more sternly; he must learn to resist the temptation to rise to every challenge. There was not enough time to play games. Impatient with himself, he returned eagerly to his experiments, attempting to produce higher and ever higher voltages. He would permit nothing to interrupt him, he said. He worked with a sort of desperate intensity, allowing a scant two hours nightly for sleep.

But his work along these pioneering lines was destined to be interrupted. Around the comer, less than two blocks away from his laboratory, in the offices of the Edison General Electric Company, concern was rapidly building into consternation, or Westinghouse announced that, with the castings for the new dynamos now completed, his company was prepared to deliver alternating current to cities and towns throughout the United States. The financiers who had invested heavily in Edison's direct current dynamos and installations realized that much of their company's equipment would become obsolete if alternating current were to be accorded general acceptance by the public. A meeting was called at the Edison office and a group of solemn faced gentlemen gathered around the long conference table to discuss possible plans of action.

Thomas Edison's gaze slowly scanned the faces of his board of directors. He brushed aside the unruly lock of hair that so often fell across his forehead, and grinned.

"There's one thing we can do, gentlemen," he said. "It may sound a little melodramatic, but I think it'd work. If we're agreed that desperate measures are necessary—"

He looked from one to another questioningly.

Everyone nodded.

Tesla stood beside his table desk in the office adjoining his laboratory, his long, tapering fingers drumming nervously on the worn surface of the desk. The bluish light cast by the experimental fluorescent tubing that illuminated the office deepened the shadows under his eyes and made his long, sharp nose seem even longer and more pointed. His penetrating, black eyes gazed unseeing into space. There was something wrong about the letter he had just received. Some sixth sense warned him that there was something wrong, but his other five senses could not tell him what it was. He glanced once more at the letter.

Dear Tesla:

I'm writing to let you know that we have won a great victory. The Edison General Electric Company has capitulated! Received a letter from them about two weeks back asking if I'd consider allowing them to install alternating current Tesla equipment and if so on what terms. I was suspicious at first and replied cautiously that I might be interested if the terms were right. They came back with an unusually generous offer of cash payment plus royalty on every installation job. They explained that they had an opportunity of obtaining a big contract somewhere in upstate New York and that's why they had made so large an offer. I've accepted. This means that you'll make millions on your royalty basis! You'll have enough money to found a Chair of Electrical Engineering at some university. You'll be able to do all the things you've always wanted to do.

And, of course, the Westinghouse Company won't fare too badly either. I must confess I'm just as surprised as I know you must be. I've always supposed Tom Edison was a stubborn man—a determined opponent. I never thought—

Tesla allowed the letter from George Westinghouse to drop onto the desk top. There was something strange about it. He didn't like it. The situation couldn't be what it seemed to be. He tried to put aside his uneasiness. He went out into the laboratory and watched his assistants at work, but for once he found it difficult to concentrate. He realized that one of the experiments had reached a critical point. A copper wire of greater tensile strength was being run through the tube containing mercury. If this wire proved more effective than steel wire, the whole future of fluorescent lighting might be affected, but he could not focus his attention.

It was not until much later, when he headed toward Old Tom's Steak House on Cedar Street for a quick dinner before returning to the lab, that he learned the answer to the question that had been puzzling him.

"How about buyin' me last paper, sir, an' lettin' me go home?"

Tesla looked down at the ragged urchin who had accosted him. He rarely bought or read a newspaper, but the little boy seemed so hollow cheeked and hungry and still so cheerful that he reached in his pocket and drew forth a two cent piece.

"Good appetite," he said, handing the boy the coin.

It didn't occur to Tesla to throw the paper away unread. As he waited for his steak, he opened it and glanced idly at the first page. Suddenly he sat up straight and stared at the headline that seemed to shriek at him: SING SING PRISON TO INSTALL ELECTRIC CHAIR FOR DEATH PENALTY' Tesla Alternating Current to Be Used as More Lethal than

Direct Current

Edison General Electric Company to Make Installation

There it was! There was the answer to his question, the proof that his fears had been justified! "An installation job in upstate New York," Westinghouse had written! The first Tesla installation would be used to kill.

Forgetting about his steak, Tesla at once left the tavern, almost in a daze. He realized immediately how disastrous this announcement would be to Westinghouse and to the world. If Edison could create the impression in the public mind that alternating current, because of the higher voltages obtainable with it, was unsafe for family use, Westinghouse's money and all their plans for supplying electric light at low cost to the farthest and most isolated part of the United States would go down the drain. He must stop work on everything else. He would have to do something—something dramatic that would demonstrate to the world that alternating current was just as safe as direct. Without realizing it, he headed back toward his laboratory.

The telephone was ringing shrilly, insistently as he inserted his key in the lock of his private office. He smiled grimly. That would be Westinghouse, he thought. He, too, had seen the papers.

"We've been had, Tesla," George Westinghouse shouted as soon as Tesla picked up the receiver. "It's my fault. I've let us down. It means ruin unless—"

"I agree," the scientist answered quietly. "It spells ruin unless we can do something spectacular. And I have an idea. I'll work out a series of demonstrations showing the harmlessness of our current. If need be, I'll even pass it through my own body."

"You'll kill yourself, man!" Westinghouse exclaimed. "What possible good would that do?"

Tesla laughed. "You sound as if you agreed with Edison. Leave this to me. I've been turning down offers to lecture. Now I'll accept them. I'll give demonstrations in theaters, in concert halls. I'll speak before the American Engineering Society. I'll impress on the public mind that alternating current is safe."

"If you can really work up a convincing program, Tesla, I'll try for an exhibit at the World's Fair in Chicago this spring. Can you be ready by then?"

"Yes, I'll be ready."

"I'll make a bid to supply the Fair with current. I'll underbid everyone, even if we lose on the deal. Go to it, Tesla. We'll lick 'em yet!"

Tesla went to work on the problem at once. Tackling a new problem, however, did not require any elaborate preparations. He removed neither elegant frock coat nor gaily flowered vest. He donned no celluloid cuffs. He simply stood, with his hand still resting on the cradled telephone receiver, and gazed fixedly at the opposite wall. He remained that way for quite some time as he mentally reviewed facts and data that he had stored away for possible future use. Gradually he began to visualize the kind of apparatus he would require for the demonstration he had in mind.

He was well aware that even the 110volt home lighting circuit could produce a painful shock if it passed through the body. He also knew—as everyone knew but had not recognized as important—that light waves striking the body were scarcely noticeable. The electric current used in his alternating current motor oscillated at the rate of 60 cycles per second and light waves at billions per second. He concluded that somewhere in between these two extremes there must be a point at which electric current could pass through the human body without causing pain or the destruction of tissues.

He must find that point, and not by experiment, for a wrong guess could prove fatal. The answer would have to come by drawing on the knowledge filed in the pigeon holes of his mind.

There were two things to consider: the destruction of tissues, caused by the heating effect resulting from the increase of amperage, and the pain, which he knew was created by the number of alternations of the current—each alternation producing a single stimulus which was transmitted by the nerves to the brain as pain.

Still in deep thought, he crossed over to his desk and sat down. Part of the answer lay in the nerves of the human body. He probed into the depths of his mind in an effort to recall what he knew about them. Then he remembered. Nerves responded to stimuli up to a rate of 700 per second, but could not transmit impulses received any faster than that. In this, he realized, they were similar to the human ear, which cannot hear vibrations above a frequency of 15,000 per second, and the eye, which cannot see vibrations of light of a frequency higher than that of violet light. His high frequency alternating current dynamos had produced frequencies up to 20,000 cycles per second. He was beginning to see what must be done. The visualization was becoming clearer with each moment that he sat motionless at his desk.

At 20,000 cycles per second the nerves would not register pain, but the amperage, which carried the tissue destroying power, would be too high. Tissues would be burned away, even though no pain was felt.

But if he passed these currents through his newly invented air core transformers, he could increase the voltage, at the same time reducing the amperage proportionately. He would thus have a current with a frequency too high to be felt, yet with an amperage so low that it would inflict no damage. He had worked it out! He could visualize every detail of the hookup. It would take only a matter of days to assemble and combine the necessary elements needed for a demonstration. But still he did not move. Another and even more exciting thought had struck him. If he could vary the current density, as he now knew he could, wouldn't it be possible to pass a current through the body without pain—but with sufficient amperage to furnish internal heat without damage to the tissues? He almost shouted aloud as the tremendous value of the idea grew upon him. Neuralgia, bone diseases, perhaps even cancer, could be treated if reached by a heat far more penetrating than any that had to be applied externally! He laughed aloud.

What had begun as a publicity stunt resulted in a benefit to mankind. And what better refutation of Edison's claim that alternating current was only suitable for killing in the electric chair than to show that it could be used for healing and alleviating human pain?

He stood up at last. There was much to be done, and first things must be done first. He would have to put out of his mind for the moment the working out of "diathermy" treatments. That could come later and he could present it to the medical profession as a gift to humanity. But now he had to attend to more pressing matters. He pulled the string that turned out the tube lights and, with a springy step, still smiling, walked down the long hall to his laboratory.

CHAPTER 17

THE CHICAGO WORLD'S FAIR of 1893 was the first such event to be illuminated by electricity. It was called the Columbian Exposition in honor of Columbus on the four hundredth anniversary of his discovery of America. Actually, it proved to be a greater tribute to Nikola Tesla! Not only were the Fair Grounds themselves brilliantly lighted, but all of the elaborate and painstakingly created exhibits also were supplied with current by the Westinghouse Company's Tesla motors and dynamos, using only alternating current. The Edison Company was not represented and direct current appliances were nowhere in evidence.

All of this succeeded in attracting the attention of the scientific world to the great flexibility and variety of uses of alternating current and the poly phase motors; but what caught the excited attention of the general public was Tesla's own personal exhibit. Wearing a swallowtail coat, embroidered vest, gray striped trousers, and a tall silk hat, Tesla seemed like a giant ringmaster at a circus as he made his various inventions perform for him as if they were trained animals. Since the Fair was intended to honor Columbus, Tesla had modernized the feat of making an egg stand on end, as Columbus was supposed to have done in demonstrating the flatness of the world at the two poles.

On a tall pedestal draped in black velvet lay an egg made of steel. At Test's command—and the simultaneous but unseen pressing of a switch with his toes—the egg stood on one of its ends and, after the slightest pause, began to revolve! At first it moved slowly but within seconds it was whirling like a mad dervish. While his audience gazed at it in fascinated wonder, Tesla explained to them the theory of the rotating magnetic field that was responsible for his "magic."

To his own amazement Tesla discovered that, by employing what seemed to him childish tricks, he could arouse interest and enthusiasm and show the results of his years of experimentation in such a way that they became stimulating and vital to many who had thought scientific subjects dull and boring—if they had ever bothered to think of them at all.

"Tesla, you're an amazing man," George Westinghouse told him after standing at the outer edge of the crowd that had been watching the demonstrations in the velour-hung shed that housed the exhibit. "Your dignity was offended, your pride hurt, because my engineers—all trained men—dared to disagree with you about the most effective rate of current to operate your dynamos. But here you're behaving like a small boy charging the neighborhood kids two pins to see a 'magic show.'"

Tesla grinned at him. "It's a good show, isn't it? Worth every bit of two pins. Just listen to them!"

Westinghouse nodded as he listened to the comments of the crowd surging out one door while a new audience poured through an entrance on the opposite side of the large room.

"It's like he was some god or something," a man was saying to his wife as they filed past Tesla and his stocky, bearded companion

"Thor. God of the lightning," the man's wife answered.

"Gives you the shivers, don't it?" a young woman said, looking up at her young man appealingly. "When those tubes of light come on and go off—"

"The fluorescent lights are easy to figure out," the young man replied with an air of great superiority. "He just presses a button with his foot."

"Well, you're smarter than I am. But I can't help it, I get a kind of creepy feeling——"

"It's the wireless that hits me that way. I put the earphones on and I could hear what he was whispering into that little transmitter in his hand. There were no wires. I looked. Why, if people can hear voices without wires, they'll be able to talk all over the world. It'll put the telephone out of business. And I just bought some stock in Bell Telephone—"

"Did you see him pass that current through his body?" another man asked his companion. "I guess the current isn't so dangerous after all."

"Did you hear that?" Westinghouse exclaimed excitedly. "I do believe it's going to work, Tesla. Your sideshow is actually doing the trick. We're going to be all right, Tesla'.'

"Of course we are," was the calm reply. "And now the house is full again and I must begin."

"I've seen it five times and I'm staying for the sixth!

Once more Tesla took his place in front of the audience and raised his hand for silence.

"Ladies and gentlemen," he began, "I am about to give you a series of demonstrations that will, I hope, make clear to you the similarity that exists between light and sound and power. All three great forces operate on wavelengths. By learning the relationship between these wavelengths, we are able to turn on a light by electrical power or project sound without wires.

"As we learn more, I believe that we shall be able to project images through the air without wires. The air around us is filled with unheard music. We have but to learn the frequency of its vibrations in order to be able to hear it.

"When I was a boy I dreamed of taming a tiger. Electricity has been a caged tiger, dangerous to those who think it is a household pet, but tractable and easily and safely handled by anyone who treats it with the respect it deserves."

The lights dimmed and a spotlight focused on the tiny steel egg as Tesla explained the existence and nature of the rotating magnetic field and how, by means of it, alternating instead of direct current could be generated.

With hardly a pause he blacked out the lights in order to demonstrate the varicolored tube lights, then brought them up to nearly full lighting as he showed what could be done with a single beam of light used as a circuit breaker. When a lone shaft of brilliant white light hit a marked panel on one of the doors in the room, the door swung open! Then he held aloft a thick, solidly insulated length of cable through which he said would pass 1,000,000 volts of electricity. He connected the cable to a small dynamo and threw a switch. A spark, fully six feet in length, leaped across the room to a polarized magnet on a distant bench.

"One day," Tesla proclaimed, "man will be able to transmit power farther than the greatest lightning flash ever created. We shall be able to pierce the clouds and thus create rain. We shall be able to control the elements!

"And now for the climax of this demonstration. You see this cable, now attached to the dynamo. I connect it to a generator. You will see that, when I close this switch, the copper plate which I now place on this pedestal will be melted by the power of the million volts striking it."

Suiting the action to his words, he closed a knife switch in a wallboard at his side and the metal folded in upon itself as if it were candle wax instead of copper.

"I will remove this melted copper and replace it with an identical plate," Tesla said. "And now I will pass these same million volts through my own body without pain and without damage to a single tissue!"

A hush fell upon the room as the audience stared in awe at what seemed to them to be a moment of Neanderthal suspense. Tesla held the still connected cable tightly against his body. It was still pointed in the direction of the copper plate on its pedestal, but now the scientist stood between them.

"Would one of you be kind enough to come up on the platform and throw the switch?" he asked his audience.

No one obliged and, smiling, Tesla nodded to one of his assistants, who crossed the platform and stood silently with his hand held dramatically above the knife switch. In the tense silence Tesla nodded. The hand came down on the switch. Tesla took a step as if he had received a small push. The copper plate on its pedestal melted into a molten mass. As a gasp went up from the crowd, the assistant released the switch.

"Quite painless and harmless," Tesla said placidly. "Now would anyone in the audience care to try it? I assure you—"

"I will." A young man spoke up in a voice that squeaked with excitement.

"Oh Walter, you mustn't!" The lady with him shrieked. "The man is probably wearing some sort of clothes that protect him."

"He wouldn't do it to people if it were dangerous," the volunteer pointed out.

"Quite true," Tesla answered and the brave young man stepped up on the platform and allowed the experiment to be repeated. There were cheers from the audience as he stepped down from the platform.

"Now you can tell your friends that a million volts of intercontinental electricity have passed through your body without causing the slightest pain."

"And don't think I won't," the young man answered with a grin. "Everybody I know back home is going to hear about this!"

Tesla glanced at Westinghouse, who was mopping his perspiring forehead, and the two friends exchanged a satisfied smile. This kind of demonstration would do wonders in overcoming the prejudice their rivals had created.

A few days later Tesla read in one of the daily newspapers of a contest that had just been thrown open to the public. A company calling itself tile Cataract Construction Company announced that it was offering a thousand fold prize for the best and most practical plan for harnessing Niagara Falls, Tesla sought out Westinghouse at once. He was as excited as a little boy who had just seen an announcement of a contest in which the prize was a Shetland pony.

"Look at this," he said, thrusting the newspaper at Westinghouse. "Let's submit a plan, shall we?"

"I don't like the looks of this, Tesla," Westinghouse objected, handing back the paper. "Looks to me as if somebody's trying to get about a hundred thousand dollars' worth of information for three thousand dollars. Forget it."

"I want to enter it, Westinghouse. You know, I once told my father I'd harness Niagara, and here is a chance to make good my boast. I can do it too. The total energy supply of the Falls is estimated at somewhere between four million and nine million horsepower. Think of it! No water wheel can possibly handle it. I've always known that. But water wheels can drive a dynamo and the dynamo can generate the electricity. But only the Tesla system can handle that big a load. You own it now. I can't do it without your permission. Will you let me try it, Westinghouse?"

An amused smile quirked the corners of George Westinghouse's lips. "Tell you what we'll do, Tesla. We'll wait this one out. No reputable electrical concern is going to compete in this ridiculous contest. I'll bet you any sum you name that no acceptable plans will be submitted. We'll wait till the contest fizzles out and then we'll submit a plan with a bid for the contract."

"But the article in the paper . . ." Tesla sputtered. "It says there that the judges of the contest offer as a hint to contestants that they prefer direct current to alternating. What if Edison General Electric—"

"They won't if we don't. Play poker, Tesla. Bluff out your hand. I have an idea you're not too bad at that. Remember that horsepower deal you bluffed me into?" He looked like a mischievous boy as he gave Tesla a friendly jab in the ribs.

Time proved that Westinghouse was right. The plans submitted in the contest proved valueless, and a year later bids for the project were requested from the two major companies. And at this time Tesla enjoyed a great personal triumph when his rival was forced to concede that direct current could not handle such a tremendous load of electricity. Before submitting an estimate, Edison leased from Westinghouse the right to use the Tesla poly phase alternating current system. Thus both competitors presented plans in which only Tesla equipment would be used.

The satisfaction Nikola Tesla derived from the victory over Edison was distinctly human and understandable, but actually it proved to be the first chink in his superman's armor. If he could derive pleasure from Edison's having to "eat crow," he could be hurt by the opinion and actions of others. He was no longer the absolute scientist, living in an isolated world of creation and invention. Thus in his moment of greatest triumph, he allowed himself to become vulnerable, opening the door to the possibility of defeat.

The contracts for the Niagara project were assigned to both companies. Westinghouse Electric contracted to build the powerhouse at Niagara Falls; Edison General Electric was selected to transmit the power generated. In the year 1895 Westinghouse finished construction of the powerhouse and it stood, almost out of sight below the Falls, as the greatest engineering feat accomplished anywhere in the world up to that time. A year later Edison's company completed the transmission system. For the first time power was transmitted twenty two miles, from Niagara Falls to Buffalo.

When both public and engineers were given positive proof of the feasibility of the Tesla power system. Westinghouse was authorized to build seven additional generating units at the Falls which were so powerful that the 50,000 horsepower they developed was sufficient to furnish light and power to New York City.

Immediately similar power stations were ordered for New York itself to operate its elevated railway and subways systems. Within a year cities all over the United States were authorizing the building of powerhouses for Tesla equipment. Alternating current was at last accepted as more economical and more flexible in its varied uses than direct, particularly since alter noting could be transformed into direct current, whereas the reverse was not true.

Engineers everywhere hailed Tesla's power system as "the most tremendous event in all engineering history." "Tesla," they agreed, "has contributed more to electrical science than any man up to this time."

During the year 1891, Tesla had often thought about his father and wished he were alive to witness the fulfillment of his son's promise to harness Niagara. Thinking of his father made him homesick. He wanted to return to Go spic, to see his mother and Marica. He decided to accept the invitations he had previously rejected to lecture abroad.

With customary thoroughness he prepared a different lecture for each engagement, each with its complete set of demonstrations to be performed on the lecture platform. His first London lecture before the Institution of Electrical Engineers on February 3, 1892, took the English press as well as the English scientists by storm. He was scheduled to lecture first in Paris, then in Budapest, after which he would take a short vacation, either at Go spic or Smilax, wherever his mother preferred to be. But in Paris something occurred which changed his plans.

In the midst of a demonstration he happened to glance down toward the front row of spectators and noticed that one of the seats was empty. He did not think it had been empty when the lecture had begun.

Someone must have become ill suddenly, he thought, and continued with the demonstration of the transmission of power by wireless electricity. But an odd feeling—possibly a subconscious reminder of a previous experience—caused him to glance again at that empty seat. His mother was sitting in it! He stared in amazement. Of course it could have been possible that his mother had come to Paris to surprise him, but he did not think it likely. He turned away, forcing himself to continue with the demonstration. When he looked again, the seat was empty.

Under a great strain of impatience and anxiety he conscientiously fulfilled his obligation to his audience by completing the lecture, but he did not wait to receive the praise and adulation of the scientists who crowded the passageway that led backstage. He escaped through the stage door and rushed to his hotel where he was handed a telegram from Marica saying that his mother was gravely ill in Go spic

Trains now went directly to Go spic from Paris, and he caught the next one. When he arrived at his sister's home, he was admitted by a weeping Marica. The doctors had given up hope hours before.

"She—she's just waiting for you," his sister sobbed.

When he went into his mother's bedroom she sat up in bed and held out her arms to him, smiling radiantly. "What kept you so long?" she asked teasingly.

He laughed and held her close to him, thinking, surely the doctors must be wrong. She's so alive—so vibrant!

"Now don't tell me you didn't get my message. It worked when I sent for you at Prague. I know it worked this time too."

"It worked," he assured her. "I'm beginning to believe that we may someday learn to transmit thoughts without words, without wires. One person is the transmitter, the other the receiver. If they are attuned—on the same wavelength—"

She placed two fingers gently on his lips. "That is no big discovery," she said, smiling in much the same way she had smiled when he showed her his sixteenth motor. "Everyone knows that! Tell me, are you getting enough to eat?"

"Plenty, Mother."

"You don't look it. Are you all right?"

"I'm fine."

"You know, I'm going to see your father soon . . ." Her face lit up with a smile of such radiance that he would not for one moment have considered contradicting her by saying that he did not share her belief.

"Tell him I harnessed Niagara," Tesla said gently.

"Oh Nikki, he'll be so proud!" Mrs. Tesla exclaimed happily. "What else shall I tell him? Are you making a lot of money?"

Tesla smiled. "I thought you'd ask that, so I figured it out on the train coming down. I think, according to my agreement with my friend Mr. Westinghouse, I think I have twelve million dollars due me in royalties."

Mrs. Tesla was still smiling. "That's good," she said as if he had just told her he'd passed his Latin exam at school. "Your father will be pleased, I know. Nikki, are you sure you're getting enough to eat?"

CHAPTER 18

GEORGE WESTINGHOUSE dreaded Tesla's return from abroad. He was in serious trouble. Business had been too good! Following the triumph of the Niagara Falls installation, orders and contracts poured in from every part of the United States and Canada. The individual units in the Tesla power system cost a great deal of money to make, and the company had to cover the cost of building and delivering them before the customers paid for them. Expansion had been too rapid and Westinghouse needed money.

He went to financiers and banks and was told that before anyone would either invest or lend him money, he would have to reorganize and cut down on expenses. In every instance the first criticism was that he was paying Tesla far too much in royalties. No one would lend him a penny unless he could eliminate this tremendous item—which promised to amount to about twelve million dollars. He faced the choice of losing everything and going into bankruptcy or trying to persuade Tesla to accept a small amount in full settlement of all clearer on the Westinghouse Electric Company.

The terms he had offered Tesla had been made in good faith. He was humiliated by the thought of having to welch on a bargain, but his potential backers were adamant. Not one to put off an unpleasant task, he called on Tesla the very day the boat docked. Bluntly, without any plea for pity, with no appeal made in the name of their close comradeship, Westinghouse stated the situation.

The news came as a great blow to Tesla, who had counted on those royalties coming in for years. He had made commitments based on what he had considered sure income. Machines had been ordered, scholarships assigned. He had plans for the demonstration of the radio instruments, the building of a large radio transmitting station as well as a receiving station in a distant city; these had already used up most of his reserve and would require a large income for completion. He knew that without question he would be in trouble. He knew, too, that this time he could not go back to digging ditches. He would have to maintain all the outward signs of success if he were to be able to obtain financial backing elsewhere.

All of these thoughts flashed through his mind as he stood staring in shocked surprise at George Westinghouse.

"Don't stand there looking like that!" Westinghouse exclaimed almost angrily. "I wouldn't blame you if you cursed and swore, or if you took a poke at me. But don't stand there reminding me of all the things we hoped to do together."

"Did you bring your copy of the contract with you?" Tesla asked.

"Yes, it's right here. But it's not a question of trying to find a loophole; there isn't any. I made it ironclad. You're fully protected."

Instead of answering, Tesla turned and, crossing to his office safe, withdrew his copy of the contract from a large Manila envelope.

"You were the only man with the imagination to see the possibilities in the alternating current system. You were the only one who wanted to give it to the world. Please hand me your copy."

Tesla held out his hand and Westinghouse gave it to him. Placing them together, he tore both into little pieces. "You are the only man who should give the Tesla system to the world. Now you can do it," he said.

Westinghouse stepped toward him and gripped his two arms. "Tesla," he said in a choked voice, "I can't say—"

Tesla smiled down at him. "My mother died while I was abroad," he said with apparent irrelevance.

"Oh, I didn't know. I'm sorry."

"Just before she died, she said something which made me realize that she had no idea of the meaning of twelve million dollars. On the way home on the ship I came to the conclusion that I didn't either. I can visualize twelve million horsepower or twelve million volts—but twelve million dollars meant nothing to me. So you see, you've deprived me of nothing."

"Tesla . . ." Westinghouse began, then shook his head. "It's no use," he said, "I can't find words to tell you—Will you be all right?"

"All right? Of course. Are you forgetting that you made me a millionaire? I've got this plant. I've got all my models, the constructs for my wireless stations; I've got a model for a new oscillator that will literally shake the world—all these are paid for. What more do I need?"

Exactly two weeks later his laboratory on South Fifth Avenue caught fire during the night. The floor, with its heavy burden of machines and demonstrators, fell into the basement below, destroying every single unit. The building was completely gutted. Every one of Tesla's plans and models went up in the smoke of that disastrous fire.

Scientists everywhere, admirers—even his enemies and those who had opposed or belittled his work—would have understood and sympathized, had he succumbed to despair. Any man would be forgiven for becoming bitter or abandoning all further work in his chosen field after two such crushing blows. There were many who, to show their appreciation of Nikola Tesla's great contributions to science and the advancement of knowledge, would have been glad to give him enough money so that he might live tor years in comfortable idleness. They did not know Tesla!

It was as it Fate had slapped him twice across the face in a challenge to a duel. He could almost hear sardonic laughter and a voice that cried, "So, you thought you were a superman, did you? Well, take that and that! Perhaps that will teach you!"

Instead of being cowed, Tesla smiled as he listened to that imaginary voice and spoke aloud in answer: "I have done things that no man before me even dreamed were possible. My work has only just begun. I am a superman. I am Nikola Tesla."

He sincerely believed that he had brought disaster upon himself. He had allowed himself to stray from the path he had set himself as a boy. He had listened to and enjoyed the meaningless praise of his inferiors. He had allowed his emotions to guide his actions. He had valued the friendship of McCollum and Westinghouse. He had allowed himself to be angered by Edison. These were small human emotions, he believed—unworthy of a scientist seeking Absolute Truth. Good or bad, friend or enemy, he should have seen them for what they were. They, like the fire that destroyed his plant, were merely triggers—like the trigger of his crossbow.

Accepting this new challenge, Tesla began all over again. He readily obtained forty thousand dollars from Mr. Edward Dean Adams, the man who had been in charge of the Niagara project, rented a building at 46 East Houston Street, and plunged into work with more vigor than ever.

He began to experiment with the transmission of power through the earth. His work with high frequencies and vibrations had led him to the exciting conclusion that the earth might be electrically charged and, if it were not, that it could at least act as a conductor of mechanical power. As his first step in the exploration of this theory, he built a giant oscillator. In most motors and dynamos the ideal accomplishment is the complete elimination of vibration. An oscillator is exactly the opposite of the dynamo in this respect. The pistons and other moving parts are so timed as to create the maximum of vibration.

Tesla had a special iron cast made to house his new giant. When it was completed he attached it to a rigid steel post, which he drove eight feet into the earth below the floor of his new laboratory. When it was in place, he connected it to a motor. As he paused, his hand on the knife switch that would set the apparatus in motion, he realized that, if his theory proved sound, vibrations would be felt for a radius of several blocks.

Within minutes the local firehouse, the telephone exchange, the police station were besieged by frantic telephone calls. Store windows were crashing to the pavement; flower pots were falling off window sills; chandeliers were swinging back and forth. Was there an earthquake?

It was a harassed police captain who suddenly recalled things he had heard about strange going son at a laboratory on Houston Street. He pounded his desk vociferously.

"I'll bet it's that blanket blank so-and-so Tesla!" he shouted "Lieutenant, take three men and stop him from doing whatever it is he's doing. Arrest him if necessary. Handcuff him. Put him in a strait jacket, if need be—but stop him!"

Meanwhile Tesla was having his own troubles. Things had gone wrong. Whether due to faulty insulation or some other cause, the knife switch had "frozen." The metal of the switch had melted into the receiving arms, and the power could not be shut off. Tesla, aware that the great oscillator might easily cause the building to cave in, ran to an adjacent blacksmith shop and borrowed an eleven-pound sledge. Rushing back to the laboratory, he used the muscles that had become trained in his year of ditch digging to send a volley of crashing blows against the thick iron housing of the machine. So loud was the clang of metal on metal that he did not hear the police as they came bursting through the open doorway. They paused on the threshold in amazement as the tall scientist swung his heavy hammer like a madman. The casing finally broke under his blows. They watched as he sent a last blow into the armature and the machine came to a halt. It was then that he looked up and saw them. Wiping the perspiration from his forehead, he waited to catch his breath before he spoke. Then he bowed courteously to his uninvited guests.

"Gentlemen," he said, smiling regretfully, "I'm so sorry that you have arrived too late to witness my completely successful experiment."

What the astounded policemen replied is not a matter of record.

It is not surprising that his neighbors on Houston Street, as well as the Police Department, were considerably relieved when Tesla succeeded in convincing the great financier J. P. Morgan that his experiments required the great open spaces of Colorado.

With Morgan's money Tesla built a large, bare, barnlike building, seventy five feet long, almost as wide, and some thirty feet in height, with a partially retractable roof. Through the opening in the roof projected a tower more than eighty feet high. He planned to use this tower for the projection of electric current through the air.

The months of travel and preparation seemed endless to Tesla who, in much the same way that he had envisioned the rotating magnetic field driving an armature that would produce alternating current, "visualized" an entirely new concept of electric transmission. He held the conviction that the earth contained electricity—that it was, in fact, highly and permanently charged. If this were true, it would be possible to send electric power into the earth and pull it out at some distant point. It would revolutionize the transmission of messages. It would make possible the transmission of not only sounds but, by increasing the frequency of the electric waves, even the human voice—possibly even images!

In his own mind Tesla likened the earth to a bathtub filled with water. It a plunger were moved up and down in a tub, waves would emanate from the plunger toward both ends of the tub, then they would be pushed back toward the center. When they met, they would again be sent back toward the ends and this would be repeated as long as the plunger was moved up and down. The longer the process continued, the larger grew the waves until they swept over both ends of the tub.

Tesla believed that if he could pump enough electricity into the earth, the waves would speed to the opposite magnetic pole, become remagnetized, and return toward the node, or pole, from which they had emanated. Like the waves in the bathtub, they would collide with the onrushing currents being generated continuously, and this collision would produce such vast power that it would be possible to transmit the human voice on it to all parts of the world without wires—by the simple device of making a connection with the earth, thus completing the circuit by "grounding."

In creating his pump, or "plunger," in the Colorado laboratory, Tesla installed giant coils with banks of condensers and a huge mast that projected through the opening in the roof. At the top of the mast was a copper ball three feet in circumference, its base in the center of a cage like secondary coil. It Tesla's theory was correct, he hoped to be able to generate greater electrical power than had ever been dreamed of—a hundred thousand times greater than even he had been able t& generate in his previous experiments with tuned motors and high frequency wavelengths.

On the third of July, 1899—a day which Tesla later claimed was even more important to humanity than the one thirty years before, when he solved the problem of alternating current motors and dynamos—the equipment was installed. Conditions were propitious. The air was clear and cold. Tesla asked his oldest assistant, Dolman Cite, who had worked for him in the Houston Street laboratory, if he would like to handle the switchboard through which the current from the powerhouse in Colorado Springs was brought into the building. Cite was honored. Both men dressed for the occasion, Cite wearing asbestos lined rubber gloves and rubber soled shoes, Tesla donning a frock coat and derby hat. After a careful check of all the apparatus to make certain that it was capable of carrying a tremendous load of current—Tesla wanted no repetition of the Houston Street experience—he gave final instructions to Cite.

"When I say 'Now!' you will close the switch. You will hold it closed for exactly one second ... no longer. You will then open it."

Cite nodded, struck dumb with excitement, as Tesla took up a position that enabled him to see the copper ball at the top of the mast.

On signal, Cite jammed home the knife switch and pulled it out again immediately. In that instant of contact the entire secondary coil was framed with tiny, hair-like flames. Cracking, snapping noises were heard in every part of the room and from above came a great boom\

"It works!" Tesla cried. "It proves that there are stationary waves—like the water imprisoned in the bathtub! It proves that by disturbing them, changing their rhythm, we can create resonance as well as power! I'm going outside to watch. This time hold the switch till I call out to you. We'll try to let the colliding waves develop more power and greater resonance."

Tesla went outside and stood a hundred feet or so from the barn like building. Inside Cite stood in readiness, awaiting the signal. He knew that the apparatus could draw a heavy load but he also knew that with such a load a short circuit in the primary coil could prove as destructive as a volcano.

"Now!"

Cite jammed home the switch and jumped back, more than half expecting the quick flash and explosive blast of a short circuit. The coils began to flame with masses of fiery hair. Everything in the room was spewing needles of fire. There was the same crackling sound from above, followed by the thunderous boom—but there was no short circuit. The crackling grew louder and louder; the room was filled with a roar that was all but deafening. Cite realized that he could not hear Tesla's command to release the switch. He wondered what he should do. Tesla might be hurt . . . unconscious.

Tesla, far from unconscious, was in a sort of ecstasy as he watched his theories being confirmed. His visualization became reality as the sparks, which at first had been only a foot long as they leaped from the copper ball atop the mast, grew longer and longer as the energy built up until they were as thick around as his arm and bounding a distance of over a hundred feet. Each was longer than the last and each was succeeded by thunder that could be heard fifteen or more miles away.

"I have created lightning!" Tesla shouted, raising his arms heavenward. "I have created thunder. Man can not only conquer the elements, he can improve on them. He can control them—make them do his bidding!"

Suddenly the man made thunder ceased. The lightning disappeared. The long laboratory building stood silhouetted against the desert sky—silent and in complete darkness.

In alarm Tesla ran toward it, calling to his assistant, "Ito, are you hurt? Are you all right? Ito!"

As he rushed into the building he saw at once that Ito was unharmed. He was standing, dazed, before the switchboard. In silence he pointed at it. Tesla's eyes following the pointing finger, saw that both the voltmeter and ammeter were registering zero." Call the powerhouse!" he shouted, "They've shut off our power. They've no right to do that. They mustn't—"

Ito was already at the phone. Tesla took it from him.

"This is Nikola Tesla" he shouted. "You have cut off my power. You must give me back the power. You must not cut it off."

"Cut it off, nothing!" a furious voice answered. "Your experiments have knocked our generator off the line. The armature has melted like wax; the coils are on fire. You've wrecked our powerhouse. It will be a hot winter when you get any power out there, Mister."

CHAPTER 19

A LIGHTNING STROKE consists of tremendously heavy currents, many thousands of amperes at millions of volts, but it lasts only a few millionths of a second. If supplied with current continuously, the lightning flash would last indefinitely.

Tesla, in his Colorado Springs laboratory, succeeded in pumping a steady flow of current into the earth. In an hour he charged the earth with several hundred times as much electrical energy as is contained in a single lightning stroke.

In describing his work with the giant oscillator, Tesla, using conservative estimates of his results, stated in his article in the Century magazine of June, 1900:

However extraordinary the results shown may appear, they are but trifling compared with those attainable by apparatus designed on these same principles. I have produced electrical discharges the actual path of which, from end to end, was probably more than 100 feet long; but it would not be difficult to reach lengths a hundred times as great.

I have produced electrical movements occurring at the rate of approximately 100,000 horsepower, but rates of one, five or ten million horsepower are easily practicable. In these experiments effects were developed incomparably greater than ever produced by any human agencies, and yet these results are but an embryo of what is to be.

Small wonder that when Nikola returned to New York he felt as if he had made the universe do his bidding. The world was just another instrument in his enormous laboratory. He had achieved what he had set out to do as a boy. He had made himself into a superman far in advance of any scientist of his, or any previous era. He believed that, having learned to control his mind and master his will, he had gained control of his life. He was convinced that, if he chose, he could live to be a hundred and twenty years old! He was not yet fifty! More than half a lifetime lay ahead of him and he had plans for almost every minute of the years to come. He would develop further the transmission of power, without wires, through the earth. Using only a tiny portion of the power he had learned to transmit, he would develop a worldwide radio broadcasting system—also without wires. He planned to follow this colossal plan with experiments on the transmission of images without wires by means of an electronic brush or tube. And, once having achieved this, he planned spending years on testing the theory of thought transmission, from one human mind to another. The last twenty or twenty five years, he had long before decided, would be spent writing down all those discoveries that he had never bothered to have blueprinted—all the vast store of "visualizations" that he had stored in the pigeonholes of his memory.

One of the editors of the Century magazine, Robert Underwood Johnson, who asked Tesla to write the article describing the results of his experiments in Colorado, was surprised to find, instead of a cold, scientific treatise, an article that seemed wholly fantastic to him. It was not fantastic to Nikola Tesla, however. It was actually a statement of the belief he had used as a guide since boyhood. The article outlined the need for the elimination of love and friendship and other emotional distractions from the life of the inventor who, according to Tesla, needed all his energy and powers of concentration for his work. The article further explained that through automation and mechanization, the individual scientist or inventor could function as perfectly as a smooth running machine. Mr. Johnson twice returned the article, requesting the author to confine himself to scientific data instead of what Johnson considered philosophic nonsense. Tesla refused to change the content of die article and the harassed editor at last accepted it. It was hardly off the presses before Mr. Johnson and his publishers realized that it was creating a sensation. The idea of man being able to discipline himself and train his faculties to so high a degree that he could stimulate senses that in most mortals lay dormant was hailed by some readers as the greatest discovery of the era, and by others as the most fantastic nonsense.

Among those who felt themselves attracted to the theory was J. P. Morgan. He had long been interested in Tesla and with good reason, tor he had invested heavily in Edison's General Electric Company and in all Edison's direct current appliances. When Tesla's poly phase motor and alternating current dynamos made possible the harnessing of the great power of Niagara Falls, Mr. Morgan had realized that the Edison General Electric Company would be put out of business unless some arrangement could be made with Westinghouse, who controlled the Tesla patents, tor their rental and use by the Edison group.

The Century magazine article was called "The Problem of Increasing Human Energy," and the picture Nikola presented of himself was fascinating to the cool, fast thinking, level headed financier. He invited Nikola to his home. The two became great friends. Mr. Morgan, without strings of any kind, gave Tesla one hundred and fifty thousand dollars with which to start work on his pet project: a worldwide wireless broadcasting system.

Tesla visualized a broadcasting station that would require thousands of employees. He planned to have a laboratory and a station from which all wavelength channels would be broadcast. It was to be called Radio City and was to be housed somewhere near New York. He knew that a hundred and fifty thousand dollars would not be enough to complete the building and carry out its operation, but he felt that if he could make a beginning he would be able to convince Morgan and others of the value of the project and the need for additional financial support.

He was offered a hundredweight tract on Long Island, sixty miles from New York City. Twenty acres had been cleared and could be the site tor the power station. The expected two thousand employees could build homes nearby and a whole city could be developed.

Sanford White, the famous designer of many churches and other architectural monuments throughout the country, was one of Tesla's friends. The scientist now disclosed to the famous architect his vision of an industrial "city beautiful" and sought his cooperation in realizing his dream. Mr. White was enthusiastic about the idea and, as his contribution to Tesla's work, offered to underwrite the cost of designing the strange tower the inventor sketched, and all of the architectural work involved in the general plan tor the city. The actual work was done by W. D. Crow, of East Orange, New Jersey, one of Mr. White's associates, who later became famous as a designer of hospitals and other institutional buildings.

It was a fantastic looking tower, with strange structural limitations, that Mr. Crow found himself designing. Tesla required a tower about 154 feet high to support at its peak a giant copper electrode a foot in diameter and shaped like a gargantuan doughnut with a tubular diameter of twenty feet. The heavy equipment, the dynamos and motors, that Tesla desired for his plant were of an unusual design not produced by manufacturers, and he encountered many vexatious delays in securing such material. He was able to carry on a wide range of high frequency current and other experiments in his new laboratory, but the principle project, that of setting up the worldwide broadcasting station, lagged. Meanwhile, he had a number of glassblowers making tubes for use in transmitting and receiving his broadcast programs. This was a dozen years before Deforest invented the form of radio tube now in general use.

Tesla seemed to be entirely fearless of his high frequency currents of millions of volts. He had, nevertheless, the greatest respect for electric current in all forms, and was extremely careful in working on his apparatus. When working on circuits that might come "alive," he always worked with one hand in his pocket, using the other to manipulate tools. He insisted that all of his workers do likewise when working on the sixty cycle low=frequency alternating-current circuits, whether the potential was 50,000 or 110 volts. This safeguard reduced the possibility of a dangerous current finding a circuit through the arms across the body, where there was chance that it might stop the action of the heart.

Tesla at this time published a brochure on his "World System" which indicates the remarkable state of advancement he had projected in the wireless art, now called radio, while other experimenters were struggling to acquire familiarity with rudimentary devices. At that time, however, his promises seemed fantastic. The brochure contained the following description of his system and his objectives:

The World System has resulted from a combination of several original discoveries made by the inventor in the course of long continued research and experimentation.

It makes possible not only the instantaneous and precise wireless transmission of any kind of signals, messages or characters, to all parts of the world, but also the interconnection of the existing telegraph, telephone, and other signal stations without any change in their present equipment. By its means, for instance, a telephone subscriber here may call up any other subscriber on the Globe. An inexpensive receiver, not bigger than a watch, will enable him to listen anywhere, on land or sea, to a speech delivered, or music played in some other place, however distant, These examples are cited merely to give an idea of the possibilities of this great scientific advance, which annihilates distance and makes that perfect conductor, the Earth, available for all the innumerable purposes which human ingenuity has found for a line wire. One far reaching result of this is that any device capable of being operated through one or more wires (at a distance obviously restricted) can likewise be actuated, without artificial conductors and with the same facility and accuracy, at distances to which there are no limits other than those imposed by the physical dimensions of the Globe. Thus, not only will entirely new fields for commercial exploitation be opened up, by this ideal method of transmission, but the old ones vastly extended.

The World System is based on the application of the following important inventions and discoveries:

1. The Tesla Transformer. This apparatus is, in the production of electrical vibrations, as revolutionary as gunpowder was in warfare. Currents many times stronger than any ever generated in the usual ways, and sparks over 100 feet long have been produced by the inventor with an instrument of this kind.

2. The Magnifying Transmitter. This is Tesla's best invention—a peculiar transformer specially adapted to excite the Earth, which is in the transmission of electrical energy what the telescope is in astronomical observation. By the use of this marvelous device he has already set up electrical movements of greater intensity than those of lightning and passed a current, sufficient to light more than 200 incandescent lamps, around the Globe.

3. The Tesla Wireless System. This system comprises a number of improvements and is the only means known for transmitting economically electrical energy to a distance without wires. Careful tests and measurements in connection with an experimental station of great activity, erected by the inventor in Colorado, have demonstrated that power in any desired amount can be conveyed clear across the Globe if necessary, with a loss not exceeding a few per cent.

4. The Art of Individualization. This invention of Tesla is to primitive tuning what refined language is to articulated expression. It makes possible the transmission of signals or messages absolutely secret and exclusive both in active and passive aspect, that is, non-interfering as well as noninterferable. Each signal is like an individual of unmistakable identity and there is virtually no limit to the number of stations or instruments that can be simultaneously operated without the slightest mutual disturbance.

5. The Terrestrial Stationary Waves. This wonderful discovery, popularly explained, means that the Earth is responsive to electrical vibrations of definite pitch just as a tuning fork to certain waves of sound. These particular electrical vibrations, capable of powerfully exciting the

Globe, lend themselves to innumerable uses of great importance commercially and in many other respects.

The first World System power plant can be put in operation in nine months. With this power plant it will be practical to attain electrical activities up to ten million horsepower and it is designed to serve for as many technical achievements as are possible without undue expense. Among these the following may be mentioned:

1. Interconnection of the existing telegraph exchanges of offices all over the World;

2. Establishment of a secret and noninterferable government telegraph service;

3. Interconnection of all the present telephone exchanges or offices all over the Globe;

4. Universal distribution of general news, by telegraph or telephone, in connection with the Press;

5. Establishment of a World System of intelligence transmission for exclusive private use;

6. Interconnection and operation of all stock tickers of the world;

7. Establishment of a world system of musical distribution, etc.;

8. Universal registration of time by cheap clocks indicating the time with astronomical precision and requiring no attention whatever;

9. Facsimile transmission of typed or handwritten characters, letters, checks, etc.;

10. Establishment of a universal marine service enabling navigators of all ships to steer perfectly without compass, to determine the exact location, hour and speed, to prevent collisions and disasters, etc.;

11. Inauguration of a system of world printing on land and sea;

12. Reproduction anywhere in the world of photographic pictures and all kinds of drawings or records.

Thus, more than forty years ago, Tesla planned to inaugurate every feature of modern radio, and several facilities which have not yet been developed. He was to continue, for another twenty years, to be the only "wireless" inventor who had yet visualized a broadcasting service.

While at work on his Wardencliff radio broadcasting plant, Tesla was also evolving plans for establishing his world power station at Niagara Falls.

The Niagara Falls plant was never built; and difficulties were encountered at the Wardencliff plant in securing not only •desired equipment but also finances.

Tesla's greatest oversight was that he neglected to invent, so to speak, a device tor making the unlimited quantities of money that were necessary to develop his other inventions. As we have seen, he was utterly lacking in that aspect of personality which makes possible the securing of financial returns directly from inventions. An individual with his ability could have made millions out of each of a number of Tesla's minor inventions. If he had taken the trouble, for example, to collect annual royalties on twenty or more different kinds of devices put out by as many manufacturers employing his Tesla coil for medical treatments, he would have had ample income to finance his World Wireless System.

His mind, however, was too fully occupied with fascinating scientific problems. He had, at times, nearly a score of highly skilled workmen constantly employed in his laboratory developing the electrical inventions he was continuing to make at a rapid rate. Armed guards were always stationed around the laboratory to prevent spying on his inventions. His payroll was heavy, his bank balance dangerously low, but he was so immersed in his experimental work that he continuously put off the task of making an effort to repair finances. He soon found himself facing judgments obtained by creditors on accounts upon which he could not make payments. He was forced, in 1905, to close the Wardencliff laboratory.

The fantastic tower in front of the laboratory was never completed. The doughnut shaped copper electrode was never built because Tesla changed his mind and decided to have a copper hemisphere a hundred feet in diameter and fifty feet high built on top of the 154 feet cone shaped tower. A skeleton framework for holding the hemispherical plates was built, but the copper sheeting was never applied to it. The 300-horsepower dynamos and the apparatus for operating the broadcasting station were eventually removed by the engineering firm that installed them but had never received payment.

Tesla opened an office at 165 Broadway, New York City, where for a while he tried to contrive some means for reviving his project. Thomas Fortune Ryan, the well-known financier, and H. O. Have Meyer, the leading sugar refiner, aided him with contributions of ten thousand and five thousand dollars respectively. Instead of using these to open another laboratory, he applied them to paying off the debts on his defunct World Wireless System. He paid off every penny due to every creditor.

When it became apparent that Tesla was in financial difficulties, many who had assumed that Morgan was financially involved as an investor in his project were disillusioned. When specific inquiries revealed that the great financier held no interest whatever in the enterprise, the rumor went around that Morgan had withdrawn his support: and when no reason for such action could be learned, the rumor expanded to carry the story that Tesla's system was impracticable. Tesla made no effort to combat the growing rumors. As a matter of fact, Moran continued to make generous personal contributions to Tesla almost up to the time of his own death; and his son did so to a lesser extent for a short time.

If Tesla could have tolerated a business manager, and had placed the development of his patents in the hands of a businessman, he could have established as early as 1896 a practical ship-to-shore, and probably a transoceanic wireless service; and these would have given him a monopoly in this field. He was asked to rig up a wireless set on a boat to report the progress of the international yacht race for Lloyd's of London in 1896, but he refused the offer, which was a lucrative one, on the grounds that he would not demonstrate his system publicly on less than a worldwide basis because it could be confused with the amateurish efforts being made by other experimenters. If he had accepted this offer—and he could have met the requirements without the least technical difficulty—he undoubtedly would have found his interests diverted to some extent into a profitable commercial channel that might have made a vast, and favorable, change in the second half of his life.

Tesla, however, could not be bothered with minor, even though profitable, projects. The superman, the man magnificent, was too strong in him. The man who had put industry on an electrical power basis, the man who had set the earth in vibration, could not fill a minor role of carrying messages for hire. He would function in his major capacity or not at all.

George Scherff, who was engaged by Tesla as bookkeeper and secretary when he opened his Houston Street laboratory, was a practical individual. He managed, as far as was humanly possible, to keep the inventor disentangled in his contacts with the business world. The more he knew Tesla, the better he liked him; and the more respect he had for his genius and his ability as an inventor, the more he became conscious of the fact that this genius was totally lacking in business ability.

Scherff was understandably distressed by a situation in which an enterprise was continuously spending money but never receiving any. Scherff wanted Tesla to work out plans for deriving an income from his inventions. Each new development that Tesla produced was studied by Scherff and made the basis for a plan for manufacture and sale of a device. Tesla uniformly rejected all the suggestions. "This is all smalltime stuff," he would reply. "I cannot be bothered with it."

Even when it was pointed out to him that many manufacturers were using his Tesla coils, selling great numbers of them and making plenty of money out of them, his interest could not be aroused to enter this profitable field; nor would he permit Scherff to arrange to have a sideline setup which could be conducted without interfering with his research. Nor could he be induced to bring suits to protect his invention and seek to make the manufacturers pay him royalties. He admitted, however, "If the manufacturers paid me twenty-five cents on each coil they sold I would be a wealthy man."

Scherff can look back today, as he sits on the porch of his Westchester home, and decide, through a retrospect of fifty years, that Tesla's plan was basically sound—with the Radio Corporation of America, its extensive manufacturing facilities, its worldwide communication system, its tremendous capital system and earnings, as evidence in support of the claim.

Scherff remained with Tesla until the Wardencliff laboratory closed. He then established a lucrative connection with the Union Sulphur Company but he still continued, without taking compensation, to give Tesla one day a week of his time and keep his business affairs disentangled as far as possible. Tesla was meticulously careful about paying everyone who performed any service for him, but this was counterbalanced by an amazing faculty for contracting bills without waiting to see it he had funds on hand to meet them. Money was an annoying anchor that always seemed to be dragging and hindering his research activities—something that was too mundane to merit the time and attention he should be giving to more important things.

CHAPTER 20

As USUAL there was not enough money.

The next years found Tesla deeply immersed in a series of experiments. The pressure he had put upon himself as a young man at Gratz was nothing compared to the way he drove himself now. Theories, ideas, inventions, come in rapid succession. More than two hundred patents were issued to him, and the scientific world reeled under the impact of this incredible avalanche—all having their origin in the mind of one man.

Whatever money came in was spent before it reached him. He always needed new tools, new equipment. Often the things he required had never been thought of and he had to buy the materials and make them. J. P. Morgan gave him money; John Jacob Astor gave him money; so did whole hosts of unknown investors. Most of them got their money back with interest. But none of it stayed in Tesla's increasingly threadbare pockets.

Each time a new invention was perfected, either Julius Ito, son of Kolman who had been with him in Colorado, who was now his first assistant, or George Scherff, his loyal secretary bookkeeper, would plead with him to commercialize it.

"At least work out some royalty arrangement, Mr. Tesla! Hardware stores all over the country are selling your coils, your light tubes."

"That is small potatoes," Tesla would reply. "That is for pygmies. I am a giant. I must give all these things to the world before I die. Who knows when that will be? I must hurry."

"But . . ."

"No but's. And don't worry. We'll make millions, not pennies! The time for you to worry is when I can no longer get the money to pay your salary."

But when that day did come, they had long since ceased to waste time in worry. They just went on working without salary.

Tesla was not interested in making money on his discoveries. He wanted only to be free—and to have enough money—to proceed along the lines he had planned for himself, developing and refining and improving the discoveries he had made at Houston Street or in Colorado. Ordinarily, his only concern was his ability to present to mankind as many ways as possible of making life simpler and more beautiful. There are only three known instances of his taking exception to praise being accorded to someone who in his opinion was unworthy.

As a matter of fact, when Tesla's associates called his attention to the fact that Dr. Galileo Ferraris, an Italian physicist, had announced the discovery of the rotating magnetic field and had given demonstrations in both Italy and England of his experiments particularly as they applied to light waves, Tesla had been amused.

"You made the same discovery more than fifteen years ago' Why don't you deny this man's claim publicly?" Ito asked.

"Why embarrass the man?" Tesla replied. "He probably needs to impress the English in order to obtain backing for further experiments. He has come upon his discovery honestly through his own work. He has copied nothing of mine. Therefore he has stolen nothing from me. Why should he not have the honor—if there is honor connected with such a discovery?"

But later, when Tesla made a second lecture trip abroad and discovered that to the English, according to English newspapers, he was merely an imitator of Ferraris, attempting to detract from the Italian's fame, he became indignant and forcefully denied that he was in any sense an imitator. He was able to document his claims so completely that the English newspapers were compelled to print a somewhat grudging and ungracious retraction.

Although there was nothing personal in his feeling, Tesla resented Albert Einstein. In 1905, when still in his middle twenties, young Einstein had published an article in the Prague Annals of Physics announcing his famous $E = mc^2$ formula, which indicated that there was energy in matter. Ever since Tesla's boyhood when he had told his father, with all the positiveness of youth, that he did not believe in a life after death or the existence of spirit in dust or energy in matter, he had believed that energy could be created only by live or living organisms or matter. He had energized the earth in Colorado. He did not believe that it had contained energy before he pumped electrons into it. To admit the truth of Einstein's theory would have been to proclaim his own error. Humanly and quite understandably, he shut his ears and mind against those who hailed the new theory of relativity.

"I have pumped millions of electrons into the earth. I have produced streams of atoms. Never has one been 'smashed.' Never has one created an explosion!"

There was another reason for his refusal to believe in the theory of relativity. It claimed that all truth was relative, dependent upon the point of view of the observer. Nikola Tesla believed that there was an Absolute Truth in a mechanized universe in which man could be developed into the perfect machine if he could succeed in eliminating emotional distractions from his life. He was determined to ignore the possibility of error in this thinking. He had spent the greater part of his life in an attempt to prove his own theory.

The third exception to Tesla's general attitude of mild disinterest where other scientists were concerned, was Thomas Alva Edison. To Tesla, Edison was a fumbling trial-and-error man instead of a scientist. As far as Tesla was concerned, Edison's lack of formal education did not indicate the Yankee get-up-and-go spirit that served to endear Edison to the public. On the contrary, it eliminated him from Tesla's mind as deserving of the name of "scientist." Tesla could not forget that he himself had spent nearly twenty years in the Normal School, the Real Gymnasium, the Higher Real Gymnasium, the Polytechnic Institute, and the University of Prague. Nor could he overlook the fact that Edison did not attempt to evolve principles or discover new theories as inventors, in Tesla's mind, were compelled to do. Edison merely devised ways of commercializing and marketing products based on discoveries made by others. He never denied that there was a great need for men who could find practical means of applying discoveries and theoretical knowledge, but Tesla felt that such men should not be called scientists or inventors.

So strongly did he feel about this that when, in 1912, the Nobel Prize was offered to him and Edison jointly, Tesla refused to be thus linked with the man who had once betrayed him, and refused to accept the prize or the desperately needed twenty thousand dollars that would have accompanied it. The prize was thus denied to Edison too, and it was awarded to a little-known physicist named Niles Gustav Dalen for his work on illumination by gas.

In 1917 Tesla was informed that he was to be the guest of honor at a dinner given by the American Institute of Electrical Engineers on which occasion he was to receive the Edison Merit of Achievement medal. He refused.

"Every time the institute awards an Edison medal," he said, "Edison is glorified more than the recipient. If I had the money to spend for such nonsense, I would gladly pay to have a Tesla medal awarded to Mr. Edison."

He was, however, prevailed upon to accept the honor by a colleague whom he greatly respected—Mr. B. A. Behrend. But when the guests were seated at their tables in the large banquet hall in the Engineers' Club on West 39th Street, there was no sign of Tesla. Behrend, thinking he might have been delayed at his office or laboratory, telephoned Ito

"No, he's not here, Mr., Behrend," Ito answered. "Have you looked in Bryant Park?"

"Bryant Park!" Behrend exclaimed. "You mean the little park behind the New York Public Library? What would he be doing there?"

Ito was embarrassed. "He often feeds the pigeons," was his reply.

Behrend rushed out of the club, ran the two blocks, and indeed found Tesla engaged in feeding the pigeons.

"No one else feeds them," he explained to the astonished Behrend. "They have come to count on me. I don't want to disappoint them."

He cast the last handful of birdseed to the ground and followed Behrend meekly to the dinner.

Money and time! There was never enough of either. He continued to draw on seemingly inexhaustible reservoirs of energy to drive himself to more work and greater effort. He shut love and friendship out of his life. He succeeded in making himself a super robot.

He lived in solitary splendor at the Waldorf Astoria—always dining alone at the same table in the corner—until his unpaid bill reached such proportions that he was asked to leave.

He moved to the St. Regis Hotel and from there went to the Pennsylvania, the Governor Clinton, and finally the New Yorker. If he had ever stopped to wonder why he was never prosecuted, since it is a felony to leave a hotel without paying the bill, he would have been amazed and grieved to learn that Behrend or Morgan or Astor or McCollum who had run the fifty thousand dollars he had received as a "finder's fee" into a great fortune, followed Tesla's trail from hotel to hotel, quietly picking up the bills.

Tesla never saw any of these men any more, there was never enough time. Always there was too much work to be done. Once in a great while, when he was sitting in the park after a day of untiring work, he would remember some of them. Once in a while he would think of McCollum, and it would seem to him that he saw in his eyes the same look that had once haunted him when he had left his dog, Keno—a look of hurt, a plea not to be deserted. But he dismissed the thought. Pigeons didn't ask for affection. They only expected to be fed.

He continued to work and to file patent after patent. The basic requirements of a radar screen, the fundamental principles on which the guided missile is operated, the lethal beam of electronic energy that could destroy a metal object at a distance of three miles—these and other inventions testified to the many discoveries that he had made earlier and filed away in his memory for development in his later years. Then, suddenly, the activity ceased.

In 1942 some of his laboratory assistants and others whom he had trained told him of mysterious offers being held out to them to work in greatest secrecy on some new project at various places in the United States. The world was again at war and it was evident to Tesla that these offers had something to do with America's war effort. His former students were loyal to him and had complete faith in his allegiance to the United States of which he was now a citizen, and the cause of freedom. They knew that Hitler had taken over Yugoslavia, which was the present name for what had once been Croatia and Serbia where he had been born. He learned that Einstein's theories had been confirmed. Energy could be released from matter. An atom bomb was being developed so powerful that it could completely destroy a whole city.

It was not only the fact that he was proven wrong that affected Tesla. It was the fact that all of man's science seemed to be turned toward destruction instead of for the betterment of humanity. This and other questions began to torment him. Had he been wrong to forego love and friendship for perfection in a science that would destroy the world? Had those dolts in the audience at the World's Fair who claimed that there was something supernatural, something evil, about electricity— had they been right all along? Had he been tragically wrong in thinking that he could control the unleashed tiger? These were questions he could not answer. For the first time since his boyhood he found himself unable to summon up the answers. Was there nothing else left tor Nikola Tesla to do?

That last question he could answer. There was one alternative. There was something else that he could do. He could prove—to himself at least—that he was still the superman, that he could still control the functioning of his spirit and his body. He was in the best of health. There was no reason to suppose that he would not live a great many years more, exactly as he had planned. Unless he should change that plan. He could will himself to stop living. If his will were still the master of his body, then he was still undefeated!

On the night of January 6, 1943, New York was lashed by one of the most severe electrical storms it had ever seen. George Scherff, working late that evening, heard shouts from the private office. Alarmed, he ran in and discovered Tesla standing at the window, his fists raised high above his head as he shouted:

"I have made better lightning than that!"

As Scherff hurried toward his employer, the great scientist suddenly clutched his heart and collapsed on the couch beside the window. Scherff went to the phone to summon a doctor, but a voice from the couch stopped him. "Put down the phone, George. It was just a spasm. I shall be quite all right."

Overriding his assistant's pleas, Tesla put on his topcoat, wrapped his silk scarf about his neck, and started for home. On the way he stopped to order food for the pigeons, to be picked up in the morning.

No one picked up the order. That day no one came to Bryant Park to feed the pigeons. The hotel maid, entering the great man's room on the morning of January 8, discovered the reason.

www.ingramcontent.com/pod-product-compliance
Lightning Source LLC
Chambersburg PA
CBHW071724090426

42738CB00009B/1873